Edward Lamplough

Hull and Yorkshire Frescoes

Edward Lamplough

Hull and Yorkshire Frescoes

ISBN/EAN: 9783337777913

Printed in Europe, USA, Canada, Australia, Japan

Cover: Foto ©Thomas Meinert / pixelio.de

More available books at **www.hansebooks.com**

A Poetical Year=Book of "Specimen Days."

BY

EDWARD LAMPLOUGH.

"But all these things are past away—
Gone like a shadow, or the wind."
—*Victor Hugo.*

PRINTED FOR PRIVATE CIRCULATION.

HULL:
CHARLES HENRY BARNWELL, BOND STREET.
1888.

PREFACE.

A PREFACE to "Frescoes" is almost unnecessary, since its circulation is confined to a small number of subscribers and private friends, to whom the intention has been sufficiently, if not fully, explained. It is, however, within the bounds of the possible that an odd copy may survive the mutations of the next half-century, when probably few, if any, of the original subscribers will be existing under the present conditions of being; and should such a surviving copy fall into the hands of a curious antiquary, the absence of a preface may cause much trouble to his soul, and perhaps originate many cunningly devised speculations, whose deviation from the truth will probably be in exact proportion to the ingenuity of the reasoning.

To obviate even so remote a contingency it may be well to write a preface, even if it be read by no other person than the supposititous antiquary of the twentieth century.

The first intention was to write a short poem for each day of the year, and to deal chiefly with incidents of Hull or Yorkshire history. "Frescoes" being my last production, I resolved to add to it a list of subscribers, simply for the personal pleasure to be derived from such an association. Afterwards it occurred to me that, by attaching the names of the subscribers to the poems, the association would be more direct, and more pleasing to myself. Considerable delicacy was felt by many of the subscribers, but their scruples were satisfied by the explanation that there was no intention to give honour, or to deal with empty compliments, the association being really to increase the interest of the book, which partakes largely of the character of a souvenir volume.

My connection with the Hull Literary Club since its foundation in 1880, sufficiently explains my dealing with a few of its lecture-subjects.

There is no pretention to fine writing in "Frescoes," the historic pictures being rudely cut, the intention being to reflect the off-hand, impulsive expression of those who were spectators, or actors in the scenes recorded.

The only indulgence claimed from my readers is that of reminding them of the bonds in which I have worked—being in most cases confined to certain subjects, and in all cases limited to a certain number of lines. Once commenced, the book had to be completed quickly, and certainly it has been produced under exceptional difficulties.

I had hoped to include in "Frescoes" a larger number of poems from the pen of my brother, D. D. Lamplough, but his untimely death deprived me of this pleasure.

The production of "Frescoes" has involved much correspondence, frequently of great interest ; and if, in some instances, I have not responded so fully as I could have wished, it has not been through any neglect, but the result of unavoidable pressure, beyond my control.

To the following gentlemen who have kindly assisted me by contributing to "Frescoes," I beg to express my best thanks : the Rev. C. Best Norcliffe, M.A., D. D. Lamplough, Bernard Batigan, J. R. Tutin, F. L. Shillito, G. Ackroyd, Geo. Wilson, H. Hall.

    Spring Bank, Hull,
        November 7th, 1888.

CONTENTS.

		PAGE
What is a Year?	Rev. C. Best Norcliffe, M.A.	1
Specimen Days	Walt Whitman	2
My Childhood's Friends		3
January	Alfred Austin	4
The Threshold of the Year	Austin Dobson	5
On Capt. Hotham's Death	Jas. Stoole	6
On Sir J. Hotham's Death	Geo. B. Newton	7
Death of Richard Hanson	John Binks	8
Greetings	The Lady Members of the Hull Sketching Club	9
Our Volunteers	Lieut. Col. H. F. Pudsey	10
A Legend of the Crusades	Mrs. Travis-Cook	11
Education and Culture	—— Hull Literary Club	12
Beaconsfield and Gladstone	John Leng, Hull Literary Club	13
Return of the Diana	Thomas Stratten, J.P.	14
The Death of the Mayoress		15
John Ruskin	F. R. Chapman, M.B. (H.L.C.)	16
Geology	F.F. Walton, M.R.C.S., &c. (H.L.C.)	17
Obsolete Punishments	Wm. Andrews, F.R.H.S. (H.L.C.)	18
The Merchant of Venice	Rev. M. H. James, LL.D., &c. (H.L.C.)	19
Through Mazes Dim	Rev. J. Billington, F.R.H.S. (H.L.C.)	20
Othello	Bernard Batigan (H.L.C.)	21
King Edwin's Lament	J. Barber	22
The Crown of Thorns	The Memory of D.D.L.	23
Melancholy	H. Woodhouse, B.A., &c. (H.L.C.)	24
Druidism	J. M. Wrigglesworth (H.L.C.)	25
The True Poet	A. A. D. Bayldon (H.L.C.)	26
Chaplets and Crowns	Philip MacMahon (H.L.C.)	27
A Memorial, 1887	Fredk. de Coninck Good	28
Dean Swift	R. G. Heys, B.A. (H.L.C.)	29
Charles under Judgment	Mennell Clarkson	30
" "	William Shipstone	31
Hope	C. E. Watson	32

		PAGE
The Life Stage	Rev. H. Lowther Clark, M.A.	33
After Execution	Councillor J. T. Woodhouse	34
Hardrada in the Humber	C. H. Poole, LL.D.	35
February	Rev. Richard Wilton	36
England's Fame	Col. W. E. Goddard	37
Production	Wm. Saunders	38
The Migration of Myths	Rev. Sir G. W. Cox, Bart.	39
Pre-historic Hull	Joseph Temple	40
Settlers and Danes	W. Bingley, junr.	41
Our Sister-Land	J. J. Sheahan	42
The Pict's Wall	Ald. S. Woodhouse, F.R.H.S.	43
Grave-side Thoughts	The Memory of W. C. Denniss	44
Music	Richard Toogood	45
Danes in the Humber	W. Bethell, J.P.	46
Mediæval Hull	Alfred H. Young	47
Our Advocates	Edwin G. Eeles	48
Not Lost	Rev. Geo. Robinson	49
The Income Tax	Alderman Seaton	50
The Effect of Climate	J. W. Mason, M.B., M.C., M.R.C.S.	51
Clubs	Ald. Fraser, M.R.C.S.	52
The de la Poles	Rev. Canon Kemp, M.A.	53
The Cousins	R. M. and E. G. Bell	54
Bonds and Fetters	J. Rymer Young	55
Six Days on a Mast	Mrs. M. H. Newton	56
A Trip to the Cape	Wm. Wilkinson	57
W. Blake	Rev J. T. Freeth	58
The Death of Wolfe	Geo. Lancaster	59
Vows of Chivalry	E. Lamplough	60
The Tempest	Thos. Brogden	61
Death of Northumberland	Major Clarke	62
Longfellow	John H. Leggott, F.R.H.S.	63
Sir Arthur Helps	Rev. J. W. Crake	64
Argentine	Miss Cook	65
March	Mrs. G. M. Tweddell	66
A Memorial	Joseph Hatton	67
A Tail-piece	T. Tindall Wildridge	68
Three Indian Cities	Capt. J. Campbell-Thomson, C.E.	69
Staffordshire War-Placques	W. H. Hatton	70
Quite Ready	The Memory of Nelly Bruce	71
The Cid	Charles Mason	72
Father Matthews	Edmund Wrigglesworth	73
Cochrane at Lauder Bridge	W. Tirebuck	74
Warenne's Tenure	C. Staniland Wake	75
Earl Gowrie at Dundee	David Maxwell	76

			PAGE
Fair Rosamond	Thos. Walton, M.R.C.S., F.C.S. &c.		77
The Question	J. Alexander, M.R.C.S.		78
Edward IV. Shut Out	Geo. P. Craven		79
Dawson the Artist	J. Potter Briscoe, F.R.H.S.		80
Hotham Demands Admission	Samuel Davis		81
Bookseller's Signs	W. G. B. Page		82
Henrietta at Bridlington	F. R. Carter		83
A Memorial (E.C.H L)	Mrs. E. Lamplough		84
The Drama	Sidney W. Clarke		85
Hotham Demands Admission	James Rusby, F.R.H.S.		86
Spring	Rev. R. Jones		87
The Pen	John Linford, F.C.S.		88
A Catalogue of Books	James Miles		89
Epidemic Diseases	W. Holder, M.R.C.S.		90
Yorkshire Place Names	Thomas Holderness		91
Trichinus Spirilis	J. W. Fraser, M.R.C.S.		92
Public Opinion	W. Hunt		93
Hotham Demands Admission	Edward H. Garbett		94
Cameos	Rev. H. W. Perris		95
History and Poetry	S. Harris		96
A Tour in Norway	C. H. Milburn, M.B.		97
April	G. Markham Tweddell		98
The Massacre at York	Samuel Waddington		99
The Fate of Lord Clifford	Dr. G. H. Crowther, M.S.A.		100
The Cell on the Moor	Geo. Bohn, C.E.		101
Friendship	An Old Friend (E.L.)		102
Germany's Struggle	G. Krause, P.H., D.		103
A Spirit-Wreath	My Mother		104
Spring Frescoes	Dr. C. F. Forshaw, F.R.M.S., F.G.S.		105
All Saints, Driffield	Rev. Canon Newton, M.A.		106
High Church Closed	Rev. Canon McCormick		107
Dreams at Howden	Rev. W. Hutchinson, M.A.		108
Forest Leaves	Rev. T. Parkinson, F.R.H.S.		109
The Fight at Selby	John H. Wurtzburg		110
News from Selby	C. H. Marriott, J.P.		111
Yorkshire Scenes	William Smith, F.S.A.S.		112
In the City	Will. Carleton		113
The Old Home Road	G. H. Lennard		114
Revolt	R. S. Pickering		115
Through Nature	Claude Leatham		116
Sanctuary at Beverley	Rev. H. E. Nolloth, B.D.		117
The Field of Towton	John R. Cordingley		118
A Book of Poems	Ellinor Lamplough		119

			PAGE
Then and Now	Cuthbert Bede		120
Charles I. at Hull	Rev. J. L Saywell, F.R.H.S.		121
The Duke of York at Hull	F. W. Pattison		122
The Herald at the Gate	Alfred Denniss		123
A Memorial	Edie		124
Legend of Watton Abbey	James Lister		125
A Remonstrance	W. Hill		126
Easington	John Ombler		127
Barbara	Miss Louise Elliott		128
May	Mrs. S. K. Phillips		129
Love and Grief	Rev. F. L. Shillito		130
Ald. W. Gee	J. B. Hickman		131
The Drama	H. Rose		132
Aurora	J. R. Tutin		133
Prince Olave	J. A. Duesbury		134
The Spanish Invasion	C. A. Federer, L.C.P.		135
The Numismatist	Councillor C. E. Fewster		136
Loans for Charles I.	J. Malcolm		137
Mayor and Archbishop	R. Leslie Armstrong		138
The Vicar of Cave	T. W. Clarke		139
Hull Shipping	J. Suddaby		140
Home from Sea	Wm. Lamplough		141
The Ministry of Flowers	Rev. Hilderic Friend, F.L.S		142
Historic Yorkshire	Wm. Andrews, F.R.H.S.		143
Ald. Fountain	Mrs. Gleadow		144
Strafford's Death	E. Collishaw		145
Charles Frost, F.S.A.	Percival Frost		146
Capt. Edward Lake	Heneage Ferraby		147
Saer de Sutton	Joseph Soulsby		148
Old Kilnsea Church	Daniel Dunn		149
The Answer	Miss Mary Dunn		150
A Tour in Ireland	W. R. Christie		151
Pirates of the Humber	T. J. Monkman		152
Notes on Shorthand	J. W. Gould		153
Sally on Beverley	Miss A. M. Blythe Robinson		154
Ravenspurn	Capt. J. Travis-Cook		155
Popish Recusants	T. Brocklehurst		156
Hull Witches	Thos. Norman		157
Walton Hall	J. A. Bray		158
The Restoration	Markham Spofforth		159
Recollections of Hull	Rev. James Sibree		160
June	Patty Honeywood		161
Rambles and Musings	G. R. Waller		162
At the Threshold	Elsie Cook		163

Scarborough	Mrs. T. Tindall Wildridge	164
York Blockaded	George Knott	165
Gregory the Obstinate	Councillor J. T. Smith	166
The Walls of Hull	W. H. Ingram	167
At Hull Bridge	Col. B. B. Haworth-Booth	168
Sir Robert Hildyard	Councillor J. Brown	169
Death of Scroope	T. M. Fallow, M.A.	170
The Pilgrimage of Grace	Jos. Gregson	171
Belle Vue Terrace	Clements Good	172
Earl Lincoln's Death	James Yates	173
Our Lost Babes	W. J. C. Nibbs	174
A Memorial	Aaron Smith	175
Sir John Meldrum	W. Smith, F.S.A.S.	176
Death of Captain Newton		177
A Tragedy at Beverley	James Mills	178
Flamborough	W. H. Goss, F.G.S.	179
Subscription Library	Alfred Milner	180
Bereaved	C. and J. Haselden	181
Summer	Miss M. J. Tutin	182
A Summer Lane	Geo. Cammidge	183
The Peasant's War	Edwin F. Wiley	184
Earl Morton's Visit	Fred. W. Holder	185
In Sanctuary	Joseph Dodgson	186
Baynard Castle	Thos. Brayshaw	187
Revolt in Holderness	Ald. S. Woodhouse	188
Anlaf in the Humber	Simeon Raynor	189
The Press-Gang	J. N. Dickinson	190
Through the Window	Miss Minnie Hyde	191
July	J. R. Robinson	192
Bradford in 1643	James Dewhurst	193
Cromwell's Charge	Major A. L. Flodman	194
The Constitutionalist	F. Brent Grotrian, M.P.	195
John Tutbury's Defence	W. H. Brittain, J.P.	196
On Whitby Sands	Geo. Clarke	197
Landing of Bolingbroke	Lewis L. Kropf	198
Ravenser Odd	S. A Adamson, F.G.S.	199
A Memorial	Capt. J. V. Morris	200
Gladstone	W. T. Nettleship	201
Summer Frescoes	R. H. Philip	202
Romance	C. H. Barnwell	203
Prison Literature	A. Chamberlain, B.A.	204
Transatlantic Experiences	W. Barter, M.D.	205
Plato and Bacon	J. A. Patrick	206
History	C. C. Norman	207

		PAGE
Legend of Romelli	Mrs. Garnet-Orme	208
Richmond	Rev. J. Tinkler, M.A	209
Civil War	Walter Thornbury	210
The Lords of Holderness	F. Ross, F.R.H.S.	211
Dreams, I.	Michael Needler	212
Dreams, II.	Geo. Mackrell	213
The Humber Bank, 1866	Miss C. S. Bremner	214
The Royal Commission	T. Appleton	215
Service of the Shield	Maslin Kelsey Lowther	216
Forget-Me-Not	Mrs. Wm. Andrews	217
Sir J. Elland's Crime	W. H. Potter	218
Slaughter of the Ellands	Edward Dunn	219
Meadow Sweet	Annie (A.E.L.)	220
Our Kate	Kate (E.K.L.)	220
Dysticus Marginalis	Fred (F.C L.)	221
An Acorn Cup	Aunt Ellinor	221
Amœba	Dr. Dallinger, F.R S., &c.	222
Science Gossip	Dr. J. E. Taylor, F L.S.	223
August	Rev. E. G. Charlesworth	224
The Cavaliers	Jas. Baynes, F.R.M.S	225
At Riccall, 1875	Thos. Birks, Junr.	226
Volucella Pellucens	W. G. Tacey, F.R.M.S.	227
Queen of the Air	J. W. Whiteley	228
The Unseen	W. Pearson	229
Hortus Siccus	J. F. Robinson	230
Roses Red	Mrs. H. Pattinson	231
Prove All Things	Rev. John Holmes	232
Man	Councillor Fryer	233
The Child-World	Nephews and Nieces	234
R. W. Emerson	James Pellitt	235
True and Strong	Rev. T. Mitchell	236
Col. R. Overton	Ald. J. W. Foster	237
Primrose Dell	Bell (J.A.L.)	238
Fairyland	Willie (W.L.D.)	238
May Posies	Marion (M.A S.)	239
Beside the Sea	Miss E. Holland	239
Memories	Rev. R. D. C. Cordeaux	240
Wilberforce	Rev. W. Spiers, M.A., F.R.M.S.	241
Night	Dr. T. M. Evans	242
The Rescue	T. W. Embleton	243
Old Paths	Edwin Bell, R.N.	244
Old Hearths	Rev. E. H. Scott	245
Cutton Moor	J. B. Robinson	246
A Tragedy	H. Pattinson	247

xiii.

Title	Author	Page
Thurstan's Cross	Rev. C. B. Norcliffe, M.A	248
Thurstan's Army	Rev. R. W. Elliot	249
A Legend of Old Hull	W. Dearman	250
Raising the Standard	Ed. Dawson	251
Storming of Malton	W. Constable	252
Overplus of Blossom	Rev. Robert Collyer	253
An Autumn Thought	B. Lamplough	254
Beside the Wood	Paul Hunter	255
September	Geo. Ackroyd	256
Earl Devon	W. A. Greensmith	257
Sculcoates Churchyard	Rev. W. J. Pearson	258
Lepidoptera	N. F. Dobrée	259
Springdyke	Charlie, (C.D.B.)	260
Crabdyke	Harold, (H.R.B.)	260
The Lily	Maude, (M.M.H.)	261
The Message	Evelyn, (E.B.H.)	261
Falling Leaves	W. A. Lambert	262
Margaret	W. H. Groser, B Sc	263
The Worker's Hand	H. Hatfield	264
E. A. Poe	E. Crosby	265
Christmas	Mrs. Hope	266
A Garland	Miss Lamplough	266
Violets	Lily, (M.E.H.)	267
Art	Ed. Dunn	267
Rust	Dr. M. C. Cooke	268
Whispers	W. Denison Roebuck, F.L.S.	269
A Leaf	J. C. Barker,	270
The Fever Hospital	J. W. Mason, M.B ,M.C.,&c.,&c.	271
Enchanted Isle	F. and M. E. Haselden	272
Thomas Moore	Rev. A. Boyd Carpenter, M.A.	273
My Brother's Name	My Nephew Dan	274
Wind Whispers	My Niece Nelly	274
Heart Treasures	Mrs. Geo. Ackroyd	275
The Tower	Miss M. Mallory	275
Sunset	Mrs. Mallory	276
Shadows	Miss A. Lamplough	276
In Quietude	Miss E. Mallory	277
Andrew Marvell	A. E. Woodward	277
Hull Letters	T. Tindall Wildridge	278
The Convoy	Capt. D. E. Hume	279
An Autumn Leaf	Mrs. Erving	280
A Perfect Spring	Miss K. Hough	280
Corollas	Mrs. J. C. Barker	281
Flower-Bells	Mrs. R. Napier	281

Title	Author	Page
Wise Folly	C. D Freil	282
A Memory	Miss M. Dunn	283
Cromwell in Hull	Thos. Brown	284
Meldrum's Sortie	Major W H Wellsted	285
Amateur Theatricals	Radford S. Hart	286
October	John T. Beer	287
Knowledge	T. B. Holmes	288
Nicholas Fleming	Ald. J. Agar	289
Autumn Frescoes	A. H. Brierley	290
Autumn Frescoes	J. Gaunt, F.S. Sc.	291
A Memorial	John S. Harrison	292
The Sheriff's Exploit	J. Sherburn, M R.C.S	293
Waltheof at York	Ed. Allison	294
The Old Home	W. and S. S. Doughty	295
The Open Door	Edwin Waugh	296
Archbishop Thurstan	Rev. R. V. Taylor, B A	297
Captain Strickland	Edward Gibson	298
Pencil to Pen	John M. Gell	299
Three Modern Novelists	Henry Best	300
Home Scenery	Rev. Dr Lambert	301
At Eventide	J. and H Haselden	302
Our Libraries	Rev. J. R Boyle	303
Neville's Cross	Edward Nixon	304
Dimlington Highland	Miss Helen Dunn	305
Ad Abum	Thos Walton, M R C.S., &c.	306
The Round Towers	J. B. Williams, M.R.C.S., &c	307
Harold	Thos. Ormerod	308
Shakespeare	Wm. Andrews, F.R.H.S.	309
The Free Library	J. B. Anderson	310
Domus Memoria Digna	J. Travis-Cook, F.R.H.S.	311
Then and Now	Wm. Hunt	312
Hull Coinage	Councillor C. E. Fewster	313
The King's Banner	J. Milne	314
King Edwin's Babes	Miss M. A. Cammidge	315
Dickens	Richard Cooke	316
Edgar Allan Poe	Hy. Calvert Appleby	317
Old Laurels	Thomas Stratten, Junr.	318
November	Shirley Wynne	319
Mace and Sword	Ald. Kelburn King, F.R.C.S.	320
Eric Ericson	Alfred Aikman, M.B.	321
Plant Structure	Chas. D. Holmes	322
At Inkerman	Sergt. R. Cook	323
Tom Hood	Hy. Munroe, M.D., F.L.S.	324
Literary Doctors	A. H. Robinson	325

		PAGE
Art	Dr. John Hare Gibson	326
Northern Devastation	Henry Allison	327
Autumn	John Ganderton	328
November	Rev. W. E. Christie	329
Beacons	John Nicholson	330
From Albert Dock	Edward Dawson	331
H Giganteum	Thomas Massam	332
O Harrisonii	W. Hanwell	332
Old Memories	S. P. Hudson	333
Temperance	H. Belcher Thornton	333
Old Hull	M. C. Peck, Jr.	334
Printing	T. C. Eastwood	335
Lake Dwellings	W. W. Watts, B.A., F.G.S.	336
Nurnberg	Rev. W. J. Pearson	337
Alfred of Northumbria	C. H. Bellamy	338
Carl Reinecke	F. R. Müller	339
Love Letters	Rev. H. Elvet Lewis	340
Jarl Siward	James Wilkie, B.L.	341
Athena	Rev. James Bransom	342
Audubon	Rev. F. O. Morris, B.A.	343
November Musings	Miss Campion	344
Hidden Spring	W. Bousfield	345
Defeat of Penda	G. Roberts	346
The Water Poet	Fred de Coninck Good	347
Pre-Raphaelites	J. A. Spender	348
York Stormed	T. Broadbent Trowsdale	349
December	W. J. Kay	350
Winter	J. R. Skilbeck	351
Chinese Life	Rev. Hilderic Friend	352
Sea-Wealth	Councillor A. W. Ansell	353
Demonology	E. Haigh, M.A.	354
Folk-Lore	Rev W. H. Jones, F.M.H.A.	355
Compensation	C. F. Corlass	356
A Happy Year	M. A. Lamplough	357
Hedon	Ald. Park	358
Mosses	R. Napier	359
Old Love is Best	Mrs. Pearson	360
Llewellyn Jewitt, F.S.A.	Rev. T. W. Daltry, M.A., F.L.S.	361
Walden	Rev. W. B. FitzGerald	362
Hereward Le Wake	Rev. Baldwyn E. Wake	363
Carlyle	Rev. John Hunter	364
Portland Vase	M. C. Peck, Jr.	365
Autumn Justified	J. C. Storey, L.D.S.	366
Samuel Lover	S. B. Mason	367

		PAGE
The Norman —	Rev. H. S. Stork —	- 368
Tadcaster Fight	Rev. Canon J. Sharp —	- 369
The Question - -	J. R. Gordon -	- 370
The Reply - - -	E. A. Peak -	- 370
Lilies - - -	Marshall Bucknall	- 371
Bede - - -	James Gardner -	- 371
Eventide - - -	Mrs. Bolton -	372
Life-Garlands - -	C. D. Ireland	- 372
Autumntide - -	W. Howell -	- 373
Country Lanes -	Susie, (S.C.) -	- 373
A Christmas Card -	Edward Lovett -	- 374
No More Sea - -	Rev. W. Hay Fea, M A	- 375
Nature's Teaching, I.	Miss C. A. Reynolds	- 376
„ „ II	J. R. Wood -	- 377
Chalk - - -	Rev. E. Maule Cole, M.A.	- 378
Through Nature -	Rev. Richard Green -	- 379
Winter Frescoes -	A. E. Ellison -	- 380
War-time - - -	A. J. Newton -	- 381
A Retrospect - -	J. O. Lambert -	382
Old Year - - -	Rev. J. Chartevis Johnston	- 383
Memory-Frescoes -	Geo. Robinson -	- 384

Frescoes.

WHAT IS A YEAR?

What is a year? A point of Time
Marked off by pullies, wheels, and chime;
By Seasons, which prove it to be
A fragment of Eternity.

What is a year? Though quickly sped,
How many hopes in it are fled!
Chequered with good and ill it glides,
Knowing its low and full Spring-tides.

What is a year? All mortals sigh
To see the end of life draw nigh;
They fear the silence of the tomb,
The pains of death, the Day of Doom.

What is a year? The Christian knows—
And at the thought with rapture glows—
'Tis one more stage that he has trod,
Ere he, worn pilgrim, rests in God!

The Rev. Charles Best Norcliffe, M.A.

SPECIMEN DAYS.

A YEAR of days, bright, storied leaves of time,
Yields us the glamour of departed years;
Life's passing moods, its triumphs and its fears—
Perchance but dimly rendered in rough rhyme,
Not in that melody of true life-chime
Which brings old joys and unforgotten tears—
The old earth music, ringing in our ears
From lower realms as higher steeps we climb.
'Tis but one life from Eden unto doom—
One love and hate, one passion and one toil,
Work through the ages, with one art and tomb—
One sword or scythe to feed or reap the soil:
Thus in these days, in sunlight spread or gloom,
Bend we above our own dim dross or pearly spoil.

To Walt Whitman,
    Camden,
        New Jersey, U.S.,A.

TO MY CHILDHOOD'S FRIENDS.

These days—heroic, beautiful, or grave,
Bright with chivalric pomp, heraldic rays,
Or musical with low, sweet tones of praise,
Stirred by the trumpets of the crested brave
Where o'er the field proud, regal standards wave—
From glitter of the bright historic maze
Yield a more homely beauty to my gaze,
Beyond the flashing of the spear and glaive!
As from the painter's and the poet's art,
The soaring plume, the proud emblazoned shield,
The din of arms, the minstrel's gentle voice,
I turn unto the treasures of the heart,
And with old friends, by childhood's grove and field,
With love among the daisies I rejoice.

JANUARY.

Sweet babe! that cometh in the cold, clear night,
When Winter presses to her icy breast
The pale New-year, 'mid Nature's fierce unrest,
We welcome thee with pure and deep delight,
A vision of God's mercy to our sight,
So long by storm and tempest fierce possesst!
Our yearning finds in thee, frail, tender guest!
Dim auguries of peace, of daisies white,
Sweet violets, green pathways of the Spring!
Dear, holy babe! our passion sinks to peace,
The white hem of thy robe we bend to kiss,
And hear, as in our childhood, angels sing
The praise of our dear Lord, who brought release
Through storm and passion, with rich fruit of bliss.

To Alfred Austin,
    Swinford Old Manor,
        Ashford, Kent.

January 1.

THE THRESHOLD OF THE YEAR.

LARGESSE hast thou for me? whose heart is sad,
Whose spirit takes the tone of doubt and grief,
And waits upon the changing Autumn leaf,
To trace lost sunshine that the Summer had.
Perchance if not for me thy Spring be glad,
Thy golden, happy Summer all too brief,
Not for my joy the fair Autumnal sheaf,
Nor strength of Winter, in fair ermine clad!—
Yet shall thy Spring the blue-eyed babes delight;
Glad children in thy Summer-paths rejoice;
Age see thy Autumn-light at eventide,
And in thy Winter praise God's sovran might!—
Why should my weakness raise its plaintive voice?
All fullness shall in thy fair course abide.

To Austin Dobson,
    Ealing,
        London.

January 2.

SIR THOMAS FAIRFAX ON CAPTAIN HOTHAM'S DEATH.

Shame! he was too young to die!—
How we rode, he and I,
In the first days of the war,
Driving our foes afar!
Spurring amain
Through storm and rain,
With our riders, stern and strong,
Close behind, a mighty throng;
Counting no foes,
Sparing no blows!
Not afraid! daring to die,
And if driven to fly,
Reining in, and spurring back,
With the steed's bridle slack;
Meeting the foe,
Bearing him low,
Till the earth and the sky rang
With the wrath of our war-clang!—
Then, smiling, together
We breasted the weather!

To *Jas. Stoole,*
    Hull.

January 3.

SIR MATTHEW BOYNTON ON SIR JOHN HOTHAM'S DEATH.

I HATE the scaffold!—man to man
I'll face the strongest in the van—
Offer fair, heart or head alike
Open to attack: sword or pike
Against good buff and steady hand
That guides and governs my good brand.
I loved not Hotham; knew his fence,
His finesse vain, his poor pretence;
Yet somewhat pitied him, so ill
He bore the yoke upon his will;
Too closely watched by those stern bands
Who hold our honour in their hands.
No tears have I for traitor's tomb,
Nor blame the Commons for his doom!—
The blood upon the scaffold shed
Rests on his own misguided head:
Yet rather had I seen him lie
Afield, in harness, under sky,
Than that the axe, our Common's trust,
Should smite stout heart and hand to dust.

To Geo. B. Newton,
        Hull.

January 4.

THE DEATH OF RICHARD HANSON, MAYOR OF HULL.

Clouds o'er the sky, a bitter wind,
Adds its discomfort to the mind!
The gates are closed, and scarce a sound
Is heard within the bulwarked bound.
Hull mourns her loss! Her chieftain slain
'Mid clang of steel and missile rain,
When, with proud falcon soaring high,
Duke Richard issued forth to die!
Then Sandal saw the surges red
Around her heroes widely spread,
Heard Clifford's fierce, exulting cry
Peal hoarsely to the moaning sky,
As battle billows met and broke
With shivered lance and deadly stroke,
Where whirling arrows through the air
The mandate of the Death King bare,
And the white veil, by Winter spread
O'er Wakefield-Green, grew slaughter-red.

Cold lies the chief, in death's dim rest,
With shattered frame, and riven crest,

To John Binks,
  Wakefield.

January 5.

GREETINGS FROM THE HULL LITERARY CLUB.

You have lived—the year has rendered
   Golden grain unto your toil ;
Nature's riven breast surrendered
   The rich tribute of its spoil.
It is Winter, earth is dead,
Its leafy coronal is spread
Grey and sere upon its tomb,
Under Winter's leaden gloom.
Time, the subtle ! bore away
The bloom-drift of our happy May !

You have lived—your pencil's treasure
   Gilds some beauties of the year ;
We rejoice in olden pleasure,
   Born of April's sunny tear.
Here is Springtide's tint and stain,
Fair coronal of Summer's reign ;
Bloom of Autumn, crimson leaves,
Golden tributary sheaves,
Won from Winter's dim decay ;
Fruition of your Summer's day.

To the Lady Members of the Hull Sketching Club.

January 6.

OUR VOLUNTEERS.

Napoleon's laurels, fresh and green,
Awed Europe with their glorious sheen—
And England, held too cheap that day,
Proud, lion-hearted, stood at bay.
The bitterness of blood and tears
Rested on sad, heroic years;
The Crimea's long, deadly strain
Heralded the Mutiny's dark stain;
And grief so mingled with our pride
Scarce through the Cypress was descried
The laurel-bough, so sternly torn
From death's grim jaws on battle morn.
We had lost heroes, not dull clay,
Our grief was open as the day!
And in our grief there came the sting
Of cruel threat—so cheap to fling!
Then England armed—north, south, and west,
The bugle rang! In bright arms drest
Our volunteers, for Fatherland
In legions held our sacred strand,
Sternly defiant to the world,
Beneath our brave old flag unfurled.

To Lieut.-Col. H. Fawcett Pudsey,
  Hull.

January 7.

A LEGEND OF THE CRUSADES.

'Tis but a pillar of grey stone,
Beside the pathway standing lone,
Yet round it cling the legends grey
Of the crusaders' ancient day;
For here a baron, young and brave,
A long, sweet kiss to his lady gave,
The red-cross banner overhead,
A cloud of glory, broadly spread,
Where lance and helmet brightly shone,
And rang the trumpet's kindling tone.

Years passed—perchance the falling leaf
Fell where the harvest's garnered sheaf
Had crowned the summer-field, when they
Met in the twilight of their day,
Each gazing on the other's face
The unforgotten bloom to trace—
Perchance through mistiness of tears
To read the teaching of the years!—
God rest their souls, who through such pain
Did our Lord's sepulchre attain.

To Mrs. Travis-Cook,
      Hull.

January 8.

EDUCATION AND CULTURE.

The mind, our nobler part, we hold in fee
Through drifting time, with keen, corrective rod,
Ere we feed nature, sleeping under sod—
To see, full sighted, earth's reality.
High reason's bonds are for the only free:
With inner sight alone we seek our God,
Head bending lowly where he meekly trod,
God's son, who taught and preached in Galilee.
We little win of wisdom's golden grain,
Brow-wrinkled toilers in this school below,
Touched with time's drift, and passion's clinging stain,
Delving 'mid Winter's cold, or Summer's glow;
And holding precious to death's door our gain,
Immortal Wisdom, that shall pass the river's flow!

"*Education and Culture,*"
    By ——————————
        Hull Literary Club, 1883.

January 9.

BEACONSFIELD AND GLADSTONE.

Disraeli claims his place among the peers,
Guides and directs the war with caustic smile,
Doubts not to gain his point by art or wile,
And leads the tilt in breaking of bright spears.
Gladstone, with front that never glooms to fears,
Guides and directs, chief of the rank and file,
Smites with his iron strength who would beguile,
Sustains the front, and all the battle cheers.
Knight-errant one, who reaps the laurelled field,
And kindles to the echo of his name!
King, priest, the other, with broad breast to shield
The nation, and maintain its ancient fame.
Peers, leaders, both! their laurel we must yield,
To fade or brighten, as time justifies their aim.

"*Two Literary Premiers,*"
  By John Leng,
    Hull Literary Club, 1881.

January 10.

THE RETURN OF THE DIANA.

No flag or garland decked the mast,
The Arctic storms and icy blast
Had bleached the shrouds and cordage white ;
And as we watched the ship draw nigh
Each one suppressed the rising cry
Of pleasure at the welcome sight,
Which rose unconscious to each lip,
Again to view the brave old ship,
And welcome back her gallant crew.
For over that devoted band
Stern death had swept his still, cold hand,
And claimed as his the brave and true.
Beneath her busy deck she bore
Her lifeless master to the shore—
John Gravel, grey with lengthened years—
And sadness filled our hearts to see
The ship return, and know that he
We oft had welcomed joyously,
Could only claim our sighs and tears.

D. D. LAMPLOUGH.

To Thomas Stratten, J.P.,
    Hull.

January 11.

ON THE DEATH OF THE LADY MAYORESS.

But yesterday!—life most serene and fair,
At rest, with scarce the shadow of a care,
As flowers in sunny meadows gay
Bathe in the wealth of Summer's ray,
So this fair life—in hope and honour clad,
All blest and blessing, righteously glad,
The centre of that sweet home-life
Which makes our Eden in this strife—
With culture, love, to bless its golden noon,
Rejoiced in thankful gladness for the boon.

To-day!—the bells sad clangour, life's decay;
Time's twilight, dawning of eternal day;
The sob and sorrow of child-grief
That ends in slumber's soft relief.
Fair, sleeping child! no more a mother's hand
Shall soothe thy sorrow, and thy love command.
No more a mother's heart behold
Each treasure of the mind unfold,
And, yearning o'er thine innocence and grace,
For thee the feet of our dear Lord embrace.

January 12.

JOHN RUSKIN.

We do approach thee with a reverent tread,
In classic measure of the sonnet clear—
To all who love the poet's art most dear—
In student-homage bending low the head.
We come as guests most delicately fed,
Thy wisdom's harmony upon our ear
Making thy ethics more sublime appear,
So closely are thy words and substance wed.
At times we feel thy teaching doth impose
Too much authority upon our mind ;
Too close, too rigid, thy unbending laws,
Somewhat we doubt, yet scarcely may we find
Dissent the measure of an adverse cause :
With such reluctance Reason is to Law resigned.

"*John Ruskin,*"
   By *F. R. Chapman, M B.*
      Hull Literary Club, 1885.

January 13.

GEOLOGY.

Geology! a science cold and dead,
Buried, age-long, in driftings of old time;
The flow of music, or of rudest rhyme,
Stirred not the barren land of No-man's-bread!
It is our corn-land now; on it is fed
The strength and genius of our old world's prime;
High o'er it drift sweet notes of song sublime,
Its caverns echo to our myriad tread!
Baring its giant-ribs unto the sky
It holds broad plain, and fences stormy sea;
On the green bosom of its grave we lie,
And from it win the strength that makes us free.
Old death—new life! So, heaving day's last sigh,
We leave our progeny to work out life's decree!

"*Geology of the Cave District,*"
 By *F. F. Walton*, M.R.C.S., L.R.C.P., &c.
  Hull Literary Club, 1886.

January 14.

OBSOLETE PUNISHMENTS.

Our forefathers were wise and strong,
And bridled woman's restless tongue—
Yet not too nice, it must be said,
The bridle-spikes were stained and red.
To stop the scold's unruly breath
They ducked her—sometimes unto death.
'Twas barbarous, very; but the age
Was at its rough-and-ready stage:
Outside the gate the gallows high
Lifted men up from earth to sky;
Nor was it difficult to gain
A quick transition from life's pain—
Unless the judge was slow to pay
His visit, when disease, decay
Might cut the victim off before
The legal opening of death's door.
Such measures kept things pretty straight,
Who loved his life would walk aright.
To balance all, it may be said
Priests prayed at leisure for the dead.

"Obsolete Punishments,"
 By Wm. Andrews, F.R.H.S.,
  Secretary, Hull Literary Club, 1881.

January 15.

THE MERCHANT OF VENICE.

'Tis but a Jew! curse him, strike him,
He's an outcast! See, stern and grim
He yields the way, and takes the road!
The cold death-poison of a toad
Swelters and brims about his eye
That, downcast, never dares the sky.
'Tis Shylock, who has lost his scales,
And grinds his teeth, and bites his nails,
And ever seeks, with shaking hand
The knife he may no more command.
A long good-bye, Jew! Bless him, priest!
He leaves to-day. West, South, or East,
He'll find his lodgings scant and hard:
Sky-cover, bare-earth, broken shard
Are good enough for him! You say
Age bends his strength, his beard is grey,
Time's sunset heralds life's decay;
He's lost his vengeance and his gold,
His fair pet daughter's left his fold;
His path is desolate and cold!—
My hate's withdrawn. Your words are true.
Still he is Shylock—and a Jew.

"*The Merchant of Venice,*"
By the Rev. M. H. James, M.A., L.L.D.,
Hull Literary Club, 1887.

January 16.

THROUGH MAZES DIM.

The mind may reach unto that day remote
When Cæsar urged invasion's crimson tide,
And great Rome's strength, its valour and its pride,
The Briton met, and in war's turmoil smote.
In the vast mazes of far older thought—
The strange, dim mystery of Asian deserts wide,
Where the first fathers of the races hide—
The toilful pleasure of our search is wrought.
Nigh to the wide mouth of Time's river, we
Gaze where its volume dwindles to a thread,
Beyond the shifting glooms of mystery,
The old-world's cradle, where unnumbered dead
Repose; and scarce their life's reality
Unto our reason's bounded grasp is shed.

"*The Shemitic Origin of the British Race,*"
  By the Rev. James Billington, F.R.H.S.,
    Hull Literary Club, 1883.

January 17.

SEQUEL TO THE STORY OF OTHELLO.

Is this the end of two great loving hearts?
And shall the sorrow, wrong, and sin nowhere
Be rectified?   Shall none the broken parts
Of this sad shattered history repair,
But wrong, still wrong remain for evermore?
Will no Power even make these ghastly odds,
Nor any Just Almighty yet restore
To those grieved souls, now silent 'neath the sods,
Love's sweet fruition, for a moment slain?
Shall gentle Desdemona and her lord,
Who " loved too well," no more, nowhere, regain
The LIFE filched from them by that knave abhorr'd?
Yea: God doth reign! and He *shall* right the wrong,
And dissipate all mysteries ere long.
BERNARD BATIGAN.

"*The Tragedy of Othello,*"
   By *Bernard Batigan,*
      Hull Literary Club, 1881.

January 18.

KING EDWIN'S LAMENT.

VALOUR and wealth I see
Around me bend the knee,
And beauty bashfully
Weaving soft spells for me
While sad and mournfully
My soul still yearns for thee.
Eumer, beloved by me
Is the sweet memory
That brings thee back to me.
Prince of Fidelity!

Strong was thy love for me!
Thy manly soul, set free
So vile and ruthlessly,
My danger could foresee,
When others blamelessly
Failed, and Death's stern decree
Fell, Eumer, upon thee,
Leaving but memory
To bring thee back to me,
Prince of Fidelity!

D. D. LAMPLOUGH.

To J. Barber,
    Harrogate.

January 19.

THE CROWN OF THORN.

Oh Prince of Peace! Thy brow was torn
By the keen anger of the thorn;
But from the sorrow of thy clouded face
Shone the calm blessing of the Father's grace.

Thy hand has moved in death's dark night
To spread the glory of thy light,
And toil and wrong are fled away
In the calm dawning of the Easter day.

Grief and sharp sorrow pass no more
The sleeper's tranquil forehead o'er—
Death's passion passes in the stormy night
Before the dawning of the day's clear light.

The tears our grief and anger shed
Before our burning eyes are red,
Taking his life-tide's deep and sanguine stain
Who was by grief and wrong untimely slain.

When they whom yellow dust makes strong
Work out their will, our pain and wrong,
Oh, Son of God! in the low manger born,
Thou drawest near us in thy Crown of Thorn.

To the Memory of my Brother (D.D.L.)

January 20.

MELANCHOLY.

Not that black sickness of the soul, when hope
Obscured, the frenzy of despair and doubt
Shuts all bright dreams of peace and comfort out,
While Hate the soul gibes with Iscariot's rope!
But calmer grief, when reason dares to cope
With milder shades that throng the soul about,
And put, by Faith, life's darker glooms to rout—
O'er all Hope circling in its wider scope.
Soft falls the pensive awe of eventide,
Calm contemplation in the autumn-time,
The far-off sadness of the sweet bell-chime,
And all the pensive memories that preside
O'er olden seasons, with the low, clear rhyme
That calms and stills the passion of our pride.

"*Melancholy as a form of Pleasure,*"
  By H. Woodhouse, B.A., LL.M.,
    Hull Literary Club, 1886.

January 21.

DRUIDISM.

The Druid's pre-historic age has fled —
Time with its change has modified the race,
Whose ancient vigour in Stonehenge we trace—
Great monuments of generations dead.
Where'er we see the oak's green branches spread,
We conjure forth the Druid's reverent face;
Priestess and Eubate throng the holy place,
The sacrifice is bound, the knife streams red.
White-footed priestesses, the pearly spray
Of mistletoe cut down, with holy rite;
The Bards embrace each old heroic day
In songs that rend the dim barbaric night.
Rulers! astronomers! through dim decay
Their flitting shadows pass, arrayed in robes of white.

"*Druidism,*"
   By *J. M. Wrigglesworth.*
      Hull Literary Club, 1881.

January 22.

THE TRUE POET.

He moves within an inner world, whose shade
Our souls drift loosely by, in longing quest
For God's sweet inner-voice, to give us rest
Above the vain traditions men have made.
He weeps above the ashes of death's raid,
As when our Saviour's sorrow did attest
Death's passing triumph o'er his silent guest,
So passive in decay's investment laid.
His searching vision sees beyond life's change,
He feels the flutter of the angel's robe.
Beholds Earth's spirits its green meadows range,
And breathes the life for which men vainly probe,
As Nature with a voice most sweetly strange
First hails him Lord, then lifts him high above earth's globe.

"*The True Poet,*"
   By *Arthur A. D. Bayldon,*
      Hull Literary Club, 1887.

January 23.

CHAPLETS AND MURAL CROWNS.

Earth! thy green bosom did serenely smile
Beneath the sunbeams of our childhood's day;
Sweet blooms in gentle grace thou didst display,
Our Springtide's fleeting shadows to beguile.
In youth we loved the woodland's stretching aisle,
The sheen of fair elm-leaves in sunny May,
The lilac's cool, dark leaf; and in decay
Their glory did our sorrow reconcile.
Fain would we see your beauty's gentle crown
Amid the languor of the dusty street,
Most gracious exiles of the weary town,
In fancy seeking many an old retreat:
Our mural crown should lose its heavy frown
In garlands and green boughs, to make its grace complete.

"The Growth of Plants and Trees in Towns,"
   By Philip MacMahon.
      Hull Literary Club, 1883.

January 24.

A MEMORIAL, 1887.

Too early gone! Too little left behind
Of the deep inner life that took delight
In all that dawns upon the artist's sight,
And adds its treasure to the cultured mind.
Too few the scattered treasures that we find—
Bequeathed us ere death-glooms of sudden night
Put poesy and fair romance to flight,
And 'twixt us drew the sudden veil unkind.
Some treasures of the artist's pen we hold,
Some shreds of verse, soft, musical and true—
Wave-beaten Paull beneath the summer's blue
Sleeps in its setting chaste of liquid gold—
Some scattered sketches, all, alas! too few—
Are our poor gain from treasure manifold.

Fred de Coninck Good,
  His Danish Majesty's Vice Consul, Hull.

January 25.

DEAN SWIFT.

He loved the truth, and held his weapons bright!
No mean and mercenary toiler he,
But yielding knightly service to make free
Abused Ibernia, shrieking for her right.
Yet poor the meed of all his caustic might,
Who, like some proud ship drifting o'er the sea,
Steered no great course, to prove victoriously
What holy spirit urged him to the fight!
Fair women honoured him with tender grace,
Strewed costly largesse to his wit and pride,
And with sweet wealth of service did embrace
The strength oft turning on them to deride!
Alas, no blame!—behold the darkened face
That waits in gloomy sorrow death's too tardy stride.

"*Dean Swift,*"
　By R. G. Heys, B.A.,
　　Hull Literary Club, 1886.

January 26.

CHARLES I. UNDER JUDGMENT.

It is the victor's grace to sheathe his steel
When the stricken foe, fighting to the last,
Owns defeat, and the day of warfare past.
Wipes the red from shatter'd blade, stops the peal
Of the trump in war's wild and dizzy reel,
Confessing, with flushed brow and eye downcast,
That his banner cannot flout the war blast,
Nor one charge more his shattered squadrons deal.
Is it then the proud victor's time to prate
Of judgment, broken law, and due redress
For the crimes of civil war—bitter hate,
Red fields, battered towns, and wide-spread distress?
Let God deal with the defaulter! His fate
Rises above our law, let God his crime assess.

"Fairfax Remonstrates."
    To Mennell Clarkson, Hull.

January 27.

CHARLES UNDER JUDGMENT.

With its devastation, storm, and deep dread,
Sorrow of the weak, death-throe of the strong,
Deep-hidden bitterness and open wrong,
Be the war's strong, deep curse in sorrow shed
Upon the Stuart, its great author's head.
We are no jousters for the meed of song;
Blood-cursed, in battle-toil we've wrestled long;
Heart-seared, homicides, with hands dripping red!
In God's name, for the law, we claim this King!
Has not blood enough been shed! That's our plea—
This war's bereavement, with its bitter sting,
Sheds all its burthen by one man's decree.
Who raised before Hull war-clash and steel ring?
Who but this man? Slay him! Then is this nation free.

"*Ireton's Demand.*"
  To William Shipstone,
    Hessle.

January 28.

HOPE.

Fortune may frown, and rudely overthrow
The cherished projects of our early years,
When Hope, triumphant over doubts and fears,
Paints the fair future with the roseate glow
Her subtle hand so loveth to bestow
On Fancy's dream, that stimulates and cheers
Life's daily toil, 'till Time unkindly tears
The veil deceptive from our eyes, to show
How frail the power to which we blindly bow.
Yet when life's bitter trials on us fall,
And poignant sorrows fill the heart with pain,
Hope is the first to rend the sombre pall,
And as she reasserts her gentle reign,
We, child-like, revel in her dreams again.

D. D. Lamplough.

To C. E. Watson,
   Beaconthorpe, Cleethorpes.

January 29.

THE LIFE-STAGE.

In all, through all, o'er all, we own our God,
All-mighty Spirit! whose creative force
Works in age-labour of time's silent course,
Until plain, forest, mountain, and green sod,
By wondrous man, God's later work, are trod.
To us, oh earth! thou art a mighty corse,
The stage of our brief passion and remorse,
Whereon time smites us with corrective rod.
Thou art our school, wherein our spirit gains
Its inner calm, through storm, defeat, and grief,
And God, in sweet compassion wipes our stains,
And yields our yearning spirit love's relief,
Until we enter through life's latest pains
The realm eternal of our spirit's dim belief.

"*Genesis and Recent Knowledge,*"
By the Rev. H. Lowther Clarke, M.A., (York.)
Hull Literary Club, 1883.

January 30.

AFTER EXECUTION.

    Charles is dead !
Vain our valour, Marston's woe,
Red death-heaps that Naseby saw ;
    Heroes sped,
    Valour's head
Laid in grief and sorrow low
By defeat's dark overthrow !
Grieve we not for shivered steel,
Brethren slain in battle-reel !—
    Charles is dead !

    Charles is dead !
Now our deep and bitter grief
Knows no measure of relief.
    Right hand red,
    Vanquished head,
Curse us for the useless toil
Wresting us no victor's spoil—
No proud raising of the crown
From war's debris, widely strown !—
    Charles is dead !

To Councillor J. T. Woodhouse,
        Hull.

January 31.

HOW HARDRADA SAILED UP THE HUMBER.

    From the tall topmost head
    The Raven with wings outspread
    Fluttering waved as we onward sped
    O'er the Humber's rippling stream!—
    The darksome hours of night
    Checked not the Raven's flight,
    For the burning hamlet's lurid light
    Lit our path with a ruddy gleam,
    While oft to our ears were borne
    The sound that the warlike scorn—
    The weakling's affrighted scream
    At the falling falchion's gleam!
    Loudly we laughed to hear
    That pitiful cry of fear,
    Which was drowned in the answering cheer
    As we bade the war horns blow.
    Thus o'er the rippling tide
    We sped in our warlike pride,
    Dashing the amber waves aside,
    'Neath many a stately prow.
                    D. D. LAMPLOUGH.

To *Charles Henry Poole, LL.D.,*
      Weston Hall, Rugby.

FEBRUARY.

Sleep babe, to Love's soft lullaby within,
Bending above thine innocent, sweet rest
With strain of twining fingers, in deep quest
Christ's blessings on thy dear white-soul to win.
Sleep babe, though sullen, wailing winds begin
Their wrestle fierce, and brooding storms attest
Earth's throes of labour, ere fair Spring's behest
Charm soothing zephyrs from sad Winter's din.
Through streaming window-panes sweet baby-eyes
Behold grief of grey skies, the earth in tears,
Bare hedgerow, sodden field, and miry lane:
To gladly flash with infantile surprise
When sunshine, pure as her own smile, appears,
Snowdrops to cheer, and gild the crocus' stain.

To the Rev. Richard Wilton,
    Londesborough Rectory,
        Market Weighton.

February 1.

ENGLAND'S FAME.

Our blood is in the earth, by great deeds spread—
Our colonies are nations, and our fame
The banded powers of Europe cannot shame.
Beyond wide wave-sweeps rests our regal head;
We weave green bays for our immortal dead,
Whose triumphs touch the lion-soul to flame
Where'er our youth maintain the old-world name.
Not careful we to stain our hands in red,
Whose honour is above the upstart scorn
Of Europe's parvenus of yesterday,
Who, briefly rested from the crescent's horn,
Before the Corsican, in dire dismay
Struggled and fell, until our flag was borne
Triumphant through the last red surges of the fray.

To Colonel W. E. Goddard,
　　　Anlaby, near Hull.

February 2.

PRODUCTION.

What is the meed of this production ? Gold !
The bad man's demon and the good man's aid,
Whereby one's fitter for Gehenna made,
And draws the other nearer to God's fold.
The narrow face, so meanly proud and cold,
Is but the stamp and image of low trade ;
The open brow, eye clear and undismayed,
Bespeak the freedom Mammon cannot hold.
'Tis the world's measure of our right or wrong,
The bold usurper of our moral light,
And few there are with eyes so keen and strong
As to endure its lustre, coldly bright.
I've gold, to wrap my sin in secret night ;
I've gold, unseen, I cannot soothe the humblest wrong.

"The Increased Productiveness of Industry,"
  By Wm. Saunders,
    Hull Literary Club, 1885.

February 3.

THE MIGRATION OF MYTHS.

That common centre, our primeval home,
Curtained in mists no hand may now unfold,
Hath spread some treasure of its wisdom's gold
To glitter where Time's surges break to foam.
East, West, or South, where'er our footsteps roam,
We trace the grey tradition's clinging hold—
Comfort or treasure of the weak or bold—
Stored in the Eastern mind or Western tome:
Brought forth, perchance, in infancy of Time,
It mingles in the sifting of this age,
To make the music of our children's rhyme,
And be rehearsed when we have fled the stage.
To-day a Babel-height we fain would climb,
Yet shake not off the wisdom of some time-lost sage.

"*The Migration of Myths*,"
  By the Rev. Sir Geo. W. Cox, Bart.,
    Hull Literary Club, 1882.

February 4.

PRE-HISTORIC HULL.

Reedy tangle, hem of mud,
Wide breast of the Humber-flood;
Higher up bramble and thorn
Spread to patches of brown corn,
Scant and few, where the trees
Air their leafage in the breeze.
Here and there, storm-beaten, brown,
The peasant's home nestles down,
In the shelter of the wood,
Hidden from winter-storm and flood.
Golden gorse and grass-banks green
Brighten in the warm sun-sheen:
Wolf and boar roam the wild-wood,
Porpoise swelter in the flood;
Birds are fishing, and afar
Rings the keen axe in its war,
The forest's pride bringing low
To the inroad of the plough:
Echoes of the hunter's horn
Are on Autumn breezes born.

To Joseph Temple,
    Hull.

February 5.

PRE-HISTORIC HULL: SETTLERS AND DANES.

The harvest, somewhat scant, was gathered in;
The breezes freshened; and the foliage thin
Showed clear that autumn's work was well begun:
Swine fed in the forest, where the warm sun
Shed its soft gold upon the changing leaves—
And we rejoiced beneath our cottage eves!
The river broad was full of fish. No sail
Saw we for many weeks, spread to the gale—
When on one evil night, calm, still, and dark,
We saw a galley-cresset, like a spark
All glowing red, and with unwonted fear
We gathered wife and child, took bow and spear,
And sought a quiet fastness in the wood,
Wherein, night through, we gathered all we could.
It was the Dane! Morn saw our cots aflame,
And we, rage-stricken to take ruin tame,
Crept on their track, and sent some arrows true
To thin the number of the galley's crew,
Poor vengeance! but great solace of our wrong,
Who, weak in number, were in courage strong.

To W. Bingley, Jr.,
    Hull.

February 6.

ERIN: OUR SISTER-LAND.

Oh, Erin! island of the stormy sea,
Our sister-land, so tranquil and so fair!
Dear object of our tender love and care
Art thou, heart-held by deep affection's fee.
Thy wit, thy sparkling humour, now is free;
This boon ungrudgingly with thee we share,
And sharp coercion for thy wants prepare,
By our short-sighted Government's decree.
Fold patient arms upon thy throbbing breast—
Afar the day-star cleaves the edge of night—
From long toil of thy sorrow thou shalt rest,
Thy day is rising in unclouded light.
The people see, and to thy wrong attest!—
Our ruler's war shall be who first shall do thee right.

"*Irish Wit, Bulls, and Blarney,*"
   By *J. J. Sheahan,*
      Hull Literary Club, 1882.

February 7.

THE PICT'S WALL.

Here, cold and stern, the front of nature smites
Our human pride, and holds its vaunt at bay;
Whilst o'er the relics of an older day
Time broods sublime from those rude, rocky heights,
That, changeless, bare bold brow unto its flights,
While on their course, storm-beaten to decay,
Linger rent bulwarks of barbaric fray—
Dim, shadow-haunted of old Pagan rites.
Here burst that old-time storm of war and guile,
Strewing with death and red war-dew this spot,
When Roman valour fenced the trembling isle
Against the passion of the Pict and Scot.
Death's broad black-banner shrouds Rome's rank and
    file—
Time is the victor—Life's vicissitude forgot.

"*Picts and Scots,*"
    By Ald. S. Woodhouse, F.R.H.S.,
        Hull Literary Club, 1886.

February 8.

GRAVE-SIDE THOUGHTS.

Some little mounds of daisied turf we hold
The holiest spots in all the great, round earth,
From which our dead unto a second birth
Shall rise, when the last trumpet-peal is rolled.
Dear earth! that doth so tenderly enfold
Beneath thy living green departed worth,
While gentle daisies smile serenely forth
In angel tints of pearly white and gold—
A prophecy of holy things! beyond
The wistful straining of our tearful eyes,
Seeking with child-like earnestness the skies,
That seem to our poor faith a holy bond
Of the Christ-promise that our dead shall rise,
And in God's realm unto our purer love respond.

To the Memory of Walter Clifford Deniss.

February 9.

MUSIC.

The flow of music is an endless fame,
Escaping dark oblivion's moveless night;
The sweet accompaniment of youth and light,
A solace soft, our utmost grief to tame.
We know not the wide bound of its fair aim,
To what far region, past our mortal sight,
Its echoes quiver in sublimest height,
Beyond the level of our pride and shame.
The drifting of its harmony o'er earth
Soothes the deep sorrow of the weary heart
And lifts sweet memories to a second birth,
Some Seraph's holy message to impart.
Ah, Balfe! their fame is of the higher worth
Who are High-priests of this most holy art.

"*The Life and Musical Genius of Balfe,*"
By Richard Toogood,
Hull Literary Club, 1883.

February 10.

PRE-HISTORIC HULL: THE DANES IN THE HUMBER.

Our dark wrath-tide came! far and wide
Eddied and spread the wild war-tide.

Spread in a hell of blood and smoke,
And eddied where the fierce war broke.

Broke as the Saxons, few but brave,
Turned the edge of the sweeping wave:

Bit deep, and strewed the smoking soil
With the wild sea-wolves and their spoil.

Then the bright war-wave wrapped around,
Eddying over the trampled ground.

Echoed and rang the wild war-clash—
Then ceased the swords to wave and flash.

Over the war-ground, with its dead,
Forth from its coil the war-wave spread.

To W. Bethell, J.P.,
    Rise Park, Hull.

February 11.

MEDIÆVAL HULL.

See the old town, sleeping in the sun,
Ere the day's wild clamour is begun
Up the rippling Humber, broad and free
Proudly steers a galley from the sea ;
Making for the harbour, where the chain
Guards our wealth and freedom—won with pain :
Within its linkéd folds gallies lie—
See their tall masts striking the blue sky !
And the sheen of armour on the wall,
Where in silence stalk yeomen tall.
Here and there a cannon, strange and grim,
Threats with its silent mouth life and limb.
Strong the line of ramparts, stretching far,
Holding, with the rivers, safe from war
All the wealth and honour of the town,
Strongly held and nurtured by the crown.
Now the bell's soft music wakes to life,
Calling up the sleepers to the strife.
Rolls the strong gate open, the bridge falls,
As the voice of labour loudly calls.

To Alfred H. Young,
      Manchester.

February 12.

OUR ADVOCATES.

Great was the terror of their arméd sway
Whose glorious monuments our thoughts engage—
Palace and mosque that time's relentless rage
Has failed to vanquish to their sure decay.
The fame, the glory of their olden day,
With pomp and warfare fills a stirring page—
But did this fame the toiler's woe assuage,
And mitigate the travail of his way?
Our sin, our greed of gold, our bloody hand,
In accusation fierce and strong we hear;
And yet our monuments throughout the land
Were wrought the toiler's lot to aid and cheer.
Our roads, our railways, and our bridges, stand
The advocates for our ensanguined sword and spear.

"*Dumpty Pice: A Reminiscence of Indian Travel,*"
   By *Edwin G. Eeles*,
      Hull Literary Club, 1884.

February 13.

NOT LOST.

Not lost the culture and the loving art
That fair memorials for our treasure wrought
In mingling of sweet poesy and thought,
Old jewels in new settings to impart.
Not lost! the flashing of Death's fatal dart
No timeless midnight of oblivion brought;
Nor silence to his soul who sagely taught
From the deep riches of the mind and heart.
They who work well, the cultured and the true,
In sweet remembrance live beyond their years;
Throned by our hearths, the fathers of our race,
Young hearts with peace and virtue to imbue;
To raise the drooping soul above its fears,
Girding the nation in their strong embrace.

"*Dean Stanley,*"
    By the Rev. Geo. Robinson,
        Hull Literary Club, 1882.

February 14.

THE INCOME TAX.

'Tis bad! offended sense makes its protest
Against the tax. Its rigour doth embrace
The marge of poverty, and shows no grace
Where sickness makes its stern and sharp request,
Or duty to the full house adds its guest.
Its impious scrutiny would dare to trace
The sacred ledger's broad but secret face—
With equal doubt to plague our worst and best.
Rogues palter, lie; the true and honest pay—
Perchance the doubt and scrutiny to bear.
Thus pass the gains of thrift and care away,
To leave, mayhap, some burthen on the year—
Debt's dim shadow darkening many a day.
Who gains the least doth from his need bear larger
    share.

"*The Income Tax,*"
    To Alderman Seaton, Hull.

February 15.

THE EFFECT OF CLIMATE.

Fair Sir, don't lay it down so stern and strong,
Your moral law that holds me to the right;
What sinner can in such hot weather fight?
I must drift with the tide, to right or wrong.
To-morrow I to virtue shall belong,
Much cooler grown, and with my utmost might
Prepared to meet the legions of the night,
You'll hear me sing a more celestial song.
The weather chops to cold, my Eastern frame
Looks for some cosey covert from the cold;
But then hot blood is difficult to tame,
The warmth pervades my flesh—I wax too bold,
Alas, alas! where is my virtue's aim—
Lost! No, Sir! but deferred until I'm tame and old.

"The Effect of Climate upon Life,"
By J. Wright Mason, M.B., M.C., M.R.C.S.,
Hull Literary Club, 1886.

February 16.

CLUBS.

AROUND our Club what gracious thoughts combine,
What grand old faces through the shades of time
Live in our memory, by their wit sublime,
And find young hands their laurel to entwine—
For genius never dies! Its starry shine
Irradiates earth! Its voice, sweet as the chime
Of distant bells, now soothes our manhood's prime,
Or fires our youth with passion half divine!
Associate wit, the touch of tempered steel,
The sterling sympathy of heart with heart,
The league of triflers, with small wit to deal,
Connoisseurs in the beef-steak cooking art—
Such are some memories that to us appeal,
And in this hour the spirit of the clubs impart.

"*Clubs,*"
  By *Ald. Fraser, M.R.C.S.,*
    President's Address,
      Hull Literary Club, 1880.

February 17.

THE DE LA POLES.

Gentle and wise, the lordly De la Poles;
Merchants and benefactors of our town
Whose high munificence was bravely shown
Responsive to the king or nation's calls!
Passed has their glory! their baronial halls
By changeful time and ruin are o'erthrown:
Dust are the hands that all but clutched the crown,
Ere the last stranding on revolt's dire shoals.
The merchant was the weed! the princely heart
Beat nobly underneath its modest guise,
Nor failed to breast the falchion and the dart
When Henry's standards reddened Gallia's skies!
Good almoners were they, and did impart
Their gold to chase the grief from poverty's dim eyes.

To the Rev. H. W. Kemp, M.A.,
   Canon of York,
      Master of the Charterhouse, Hull.

February 18.

THE COUSINS.

(E. C. H. Lamplough and J. N. Bruce).

Not much between them! Childhood's happy bowers
Might well have sheltered them in their Spring-time
And cheered them with bird-song and gentle rhyme,
Amid the tincture of green leaves and flowers.
They might have built together airy towers,
From base to turret hand-in-hand to climb,
True knights, thereby to punish Bluebeard's crime,
Or shake all giant-land before their powers.
It was not so decreed—they never met
Within the narrow circle of our years,
But prematurely paid life's changeless debt,
And left us but our memories and our tears.
So they rest well, beyond our grief and fret!
Not far apart in death each small green grave appears!

To R. M. and E. G. Bell,
      Hull.

February 19.

BONDS AND FETTERS.

BOUND? we who walk with head erect and free,
Eyes lifted to the wealth of Summer sky;
Breasting rude Winter, tempests sweeping by;
Our pride—the rock that girds a fretting sea!
Fetters? who shall the iron bonds decree?
What field, what terror, shall our manhood fly?
What tyrant mock to scorn our captive sigh—
Whose rich ancestral blood enriched the lea?
Bound is the heart that frets and throbs in pain—
A sea that surges in its fierce unrest,
A whirlpool shaking its white breast of storm—
That never more shall Summer calm regain
Until there steals that long forbidden guest
Into our heart, to clasp a mute and nerveless form.

To J. Rymer Young,
    Warrington.

February 20.

SIX DAYS ON A MAST.

The form of a fragile woman,
   Bound to a trembling mast,
The wild waves shrieking round her
   And the winter's biting blast.

A group of strong men near her
   Fighting for very life,
'Till reason and sense succumbing,
   Yield up the bitter strife.

The voice of that gentle woman
   Charming them back again,
Into the stern reality
   Of their peril and their pain.

Cheering with hopeful soothings
   The weary hours that passed,
While the glazing eyes of the dying
   On her slender form were cast.

Thus, though Despair was shrieking
   Death's dirges in the blast,
Her brave, true heart sustained her,
   Six days on the trembling mast.

D. D. LAMPLOUGH.

(Mrs. M. H. Newton).

February 21.

A TRIP TO THE CAPE.

"Through many a danger and escape
The tall ships passed the stormy Cape,"
Haunt of the Flying Dutchman's sail,
Oft seen in hours of storm and gale,
Then hurricane and tempest's war
A greater terror to the tar.
Strife of the wind and raging wave
May daunt the bravest of the brave,
Where Cabral's fleet was tossed and rent
Until the three-week's storm was spent
And many a shattered hulk and spar
Bore witness to the furious war,
In which great Diaz sank to doom
Beneath the storm's impervious gloom,
No hand to aid, no eye to see
The fate that set his spirit free;
No reverent hand to deck his bier
With laurel to the hero dear:
But in requital Camœn's strain
Has spread his triumph and his pain.

"*A Trip to the Cape,*"
 By Wm. Wilkinson,
  Hull Literary Club, 1883.

February 22.

W. BLAKE.

Yea, we are blind, or see with partial sight
Some dim external forms of this strange earth,
In which we struggle on from birth to birth,
Until in our eclipse we reach the light.
Yet seers there are, who through time-mist and night
See angels, spirits, prophets, issue forth
'Mid strange, deep music of transcendent worth—
Sweet altar-driftings of some hidden rite!
Sad seers and exiles, wandering far apart
From man! most lonely when their raiment brush
Earth's Cunning and Success in crowded mart,
Where for thin-beaten gold the vulgar crush!
Yet striving, like poor Blake, with gracious art
To float some soul-notes o'er day's wane and flush.

"*W. Blake: Artist and Poet,*"
  By the Rev. *J. T. Freeth*,
    Hull Literary Club, 1886.

February 23.

THE DEATH OF WOLFE.

So many chieftains have been snatched away
In the fierce wrestlings of our arméd might,
That some heroic forms may miss our sight
In the lost ages of barbaric fray;
But never from our sight shall slow decay
Involve in shadows of descending night
The glory of Quebec's ensanguined fight,
The lustre of our Wolfe's immortal bay!
Ne'er shall we lose that last chivalric scene,
The roar of drifting battle, and the veil
Of smoke that hung above his drooping head,
His pain-vexed features waxing most serene
As cries of victory echoed on the gale;
And his last words of high content were said.

"*Social and Political Life in Canada,*"
    By *George Lancaster*,
        Hull Literary Club, 1880.

February 24.

VOWS OF CHIVALRY.

They took strange vows upon them in their pride,
Those stormy sires who kept the brave old land,
Fencing our honour with red axe and brand—
A living rampart in the battle-tide.
The sword their law, all causes to decide,
In the red van of war they took their stand,
Not slow with steel to meet each fair demand,
And wildest fury of the storm abide.
Glorious laurel and red death they won,
Vowed to strange exploits of terrific war,
Oft falling proudly 'neath emblazoned shield,
Leaving sweet love to wail its hopes undone,
And in night-dreams to wander lone and far
In search for its loved dead upon the field.

"*Vows of Chivalry*,"
   By *Edward Lamplough*,
     Hull Literary Club, 1880.

February 25.

THE TEMPEST.

Wronged Prospero! thy grief sweet comfort found
In fair affection and high wisdom's grace,
With loved Miranda on enchanted ground,
Charmed by thy Ariel, sorrow to efface;
Until the storm with pinions broad and strong,
Wrapped in its terror all the island strand.
As wisdom smote the strength of gnarlèd wrong,
And mercy sought the heart of Ferdinand,
Whereby forgiveness, through the grace of Love,
The spoil of roaring Tempests did restore,
Miranda nestling to the Prince, sweet dove,
And smiling through soft tears, all terror o'er:
Thus guilt breeds wrong, and wisdom's reverent art
Doth mercy through white Innocence impart!

" *The Tempest,*"
  By Thomas Brogden,
    Hull Literary Club, 1883.

February 26.

THE DEATH OF NORTHUMBERLAND.

In the month of storm and tears,
    While the earth was bare,
Came the old Earl, with his spears,
Blanched and wrinkled by the years,
    With their weight of care.

He, an exile, landless all,
    Striving to work out
Fame and honours brave recall
To the old ancestral hall,
    By war's bloody bout.

Bramham Moor the wild wind swept,
    Spears were in array,
Swords into the sunshine leapt,
In the van the old man kept,
    Like a boar at bay.

Poured the war-shafts thick and fast,
    Brave men kissed the soil,
Fiercely was the death-storm cast,
O'er his long, white hair it passed,
    Slew him in the coil!

To Major Clarke,
    Hull.

February 27.

LONGFELLOW.

The greener laurels of thy fame
Time-long shall elevate thy name,
Great poet of a fruitful land—
Far refuge of our pilgrim band.
Not for the classic few thy lay,
But, like the benison of May,
It gives the treasure of its grace
A realm of riches to embrace:
To teach the rich man in his pride,
And not less graciously confide
Unto the wider world of toil
The lays and legends of the soil.
More than a king, thou, poet! art,
With greater riches to impart.
A Crœsus stops his niggard hand,
His limit—but a courtly band!
Dispenser of a purer gold,
Thy bounty doth a world enfold!—
And time, that slays the monarch's name,
Serves to extend thy poet's fame!

"*The Birthday of Longfellow,*"
  By *John H. Leggott, F.R.H.S.,*
    Hull Literary Club, 1882.

February 28.

SIR ARTHUR HELPS.

A CHASTE and cultured writer this, held high
By all who love true art. Not one to force
The age to follow or commend his course
Nor one in open rivalry to vie.
In conscious faith he wrought beneath God's sky
To prove the truth, and win men to endorse,
Its claim, and turn, perchance with faint remorse,
To urge the good they might no more deny.
A councellor, whose wisdom's quiet voice
Not always rose to reach the people's ear;
Although unconsciously they might rejoice
In him, when labour's fruitage did appear.
Albeit resting from his labour's choice
Shall not transmitted wisdom work from year to year?

"*Sir Arthur Helps: a Bibliographical Study,*"
By the Rev. J. W. Crake,
Hull Literary Club, 1887.

February 29.

ARGENTINE.

Ah, Argentine! a lily pure and sweet
Drifts sadly 'neath the moonlight on the mere,
Lost in the faint May-sweetness of its year,
Ere Summer with the passion of its heat
Kissed pearl to gold, and cast it at the feet
Of Autumn, whose fruition, gust and tear
But waits on Winter's dirge and cold, white bier,
The drifting world, the grave's calm, sad retreat.
Not always is it wise to count as loss
The fading of the joy that life holds dear.
Though withered lilies counted are as dross,
In casquets quaint some hold, with gentle fear,
Dry stalk and leaf that to their eyes appear
As fair as when their Summer did the earth emboss.

"*Argentine and other Poems,*"
By *Shirley Wynne,*
To *Miss Cook, Hull.*

MARCH.

Blow, winds of March! along the furrows bare,
And breathe into the bosom of the earth
The secret stirrings of most subtle birth,
Enfolding all things beautiful and rare—
Rich buds to deck this tripping maiden's hair,
Daisies to call her happy footsteps forth,
Blue violets, sweet types of hidden worth,
To teach her soul, in sermons deep and fair,
The meek theology of earth, whose praise
In beauty of sweet flowers breaks forth again,
Bird lyrics making all the hedgerows gay.
Dear child! thy happy spirit meekly raise
Amid earth's laughter and its fresh green stain,
From sunrise unto sunset of the day.

To Mrs. G. M. Tweddell,
    Stokesley.

March 1.

A MEMORIAL.

Early they die, belovéd of the gods!
We hear the ancients' death-foreboding cry,
Shrieked to the ages, trembling to a sigh
That winds around our urns and funeral sods.
Oh, grief! the anguish of thy asps and rods
Is keener than their pain who dare to die—
The mourner underneath a starless sky
His gloomy path in hopeless anguish plods.
Oh, Death! achievement breaks thy bitter woe,
Still, nerveless hands wrought triumph from their toil.
Bending above young Hatton's grave with awe,
We strew immortelles on sepulchral soil:
And Eastward turning know that our old foe
Christ's resurrection doth of all his gains dispoil!

On the Death of Frank Hatton, F.C.S., &c.,
In Borneo, March 1st, 1883.
To Joseph Hatton, London.

March 2.

A TAIL-PIECE.

Storm-beaten cliff, wave-fretted rock,
Ye bear the imprint of the shock
   Of unrecorded time!
Waves foam and lash in fierce unrest—
White surges of the billows' crest
   Your passion is sublime!
The stormy sea, the stormy sky,
Profoundly sympathetic lie—
Lone mystery of sky and wave
That dwarfs us to the grave!

Gulls circle o'er the stormy height
Within the passion of the night,
   So sullen, sad, and lone!
One bird beside the foamy sea,
As wildly passionate and free,
   Stands on the fretted stone,
With eye that dares the closing night,
Broad wings that tremble to the flight—
A unity of storm and strife,
Of nature and wild life!

"*Thomas Bewick*,"
  By T. Tindall Wildridge,
    Hull Literary Club, 1885.

March 3.

THREE INDIAN CITIES.

PALACE and temple in strange beauty lie
Beneath the sun-flood of an orient sky,
Where the dark, turban'd Hindoo throngs each street
Nor dreads the ardour of his native heat.
Mosque, minaret, and palm, in mingled grace
Rise o'er the native's humbler resting place;
The street's bright drift of colour charms the sight,
And takes fresh beauty from the radiant light.
The charms of art and fair romance embrace
The scene, and touch it with a higher grace.
But, lo! above the fair street's shifting flow
Passes the deep tone of our western glow;
Old England's broad flag spreads its ruddy stain,
And sounds the rumble of a passing train.
The thunder of the adamantine west
Shakes the soft langour of the orient breast,
As spreads the iron sinew of our isle
The sorrows of an Empire to beguile—
The scourge of internecine strife to bar,
And shelter smiling peace behind the front of war.

"*Three Indian Cities,*"
　By Capt. J. Campbell-Thompson, C.E.,
　　Hull Literary Club, 1886.

March 4.

STAFFORDSHIRE WAR-PLACQUES.

Some battle-mounds bestud thine ancient soil,
From which dim legends, brightened by romance,
With dreams of love and war our hearts entrance,
Yielding from days of old some silvern spoil:
With clanging hammers of our later toil
Mingles sword-clash and glimmer of the lance,
Where red sparks round the sounding anvil dance,
As warrior-faces, won from time's dim coil,
'Mid wreathing clouds, stare with set features down
Upon the labours of our peaceful days—
Shades of the mighty dead, whose iron hands
Flashed ready steel to fence the falling crown
Of Henry or grave Charles, when stormy frays
Rained blood on trampled fields and sea-washed strands.

To W. H. Hatton,
    Wolverhampton.

March 5.

QUITE READY.

Ah, pretty Nelly! with dim eyes we see
The pale gold of thy hair, thy sweet white face;
Passed through such suffering from our sad embrace,
By Christ's dear love of Paradise made free.
Laid listless on the marge of death's dim sea,
Thine eyes beheld that child, all health and grace,
Quite Ready, with her dog, her muff and lace,
For the brisk drive by hedgerow and green lea:
Smiles chased the sorrow of thy weary strife,
Quite Ready, the low whisper of thy voice,
Soothed to death's silence on thy mother's breast.
Ah, last dear words of sympathy with life,
Whose sweet assurance calls us to rejoice
O'er the tired babe, quite ready for eternal rest.

To the Memory of Nelly Bruce.

March 6.

THE CID.

Yea, I have won thee, who art victor still,
And by the King's behest may claim thy hand ;
Yet bow my pride, my strength, to thy command,
And wait the sweet decision of thy will !
Alas, for my strong hand ! that wrought such ill,
Whose valour thy proud sire could not withstand ;
Its cunning foils its justice of demand,
Foredoomed to win and lose by over-skill :
Won is the dearest prize beneath the sky,
Yet may I not thy beauty's bliss embrace,
But from the queen of love, unpressed, must fly,
To wield rude arms, and of thy virgin grace
Dream through dull nights, unsatisfied to sigh,
Until, pain o'er, I press warm kisses on thy face.

"*The Cid,*"
    By Charles Mason,
  Hull and East Riding Portfolio, June, 1887.

March 7.

FATHER MATHEW.

His life was true and high, no empty dream,
No cold seclusion from life's fret and toil
In rock-girt cell, on bare and sterile soil ;
Soul centred in itself, without one gleam
Of love that moved our Saviour to redeem
Lost, fettered slaves from passion's straining coil :
He moved, a champion strong in faith, to foil
The loathly foe that dares our life blaspheme ;
With murder stained, and ruins of sweet peace ;
All foul with harlotry, and tainted gold—
Strewing with graves and tears the weary land.
Great be his honour, who, for our release,
To self alone grew iron hard and cold,
Outstretching to the stained and lost a saving hand.

"*Father Mathew,*"
   By *Edmund Wrigglesworth,*
      Hull Literary Club, 1881.

March 8.

COCHRANE AT LAUDER BRIDGE.

Mar, in the grandeur of his feudal state,
Met at Lauder Church, his peers—and fate.
To Scotland's nobles but the mason, he,
The upstart Cochrane, without pedigree;
Peers they to him, but held so rough and rude,
Mere soldier's in mind and similitude.
A Coward ?—No ! he met their deadly hate
Unmoved, and sneering at impending fate.
A rope !   His fellows, peers so rough and rude,
Sank in that scene beneath the common crowd.
"*Silk be it, lords! my tent will furnish one.*"
A horse-hair halter then they hit upon.——
And so on Lauder Bridge they strung him high,
And sternly scoffing as they saw him die,
Cursed his blind pride, nor saw the covert sneer—
All one to them did silk or hemp appear,
Save as the vulgar medium of that pride
They cursed, and had no skill themselves to hide.
Scott tells the old, grim story on their line,
Failing the rough Scot's fibre to refine.

To W. Tirebuck,
    Liverpool.

March 9.

WARENNE'S TENURE.

I LIKE old Warenne's tenure—steel blue and cold,
The forward step, uplifted hand, the bearing bold ;
And see in fancy the grave, patient men of law
Start back from such revolt in unaffected awe.
You know the story, told to-day, but ages old—
King Edward reigned, a tyrant most discreetly bold,
Who made old Scotland a great anvil for his sword,
Until at Burgh-on-Sands Death's final throw was scored.
War is a costly game, and Edward, short of gold,
Politely asked his haughty Barons to unfold
Their title-deeds, and prove that all was fair and straight—
For he was one who loved supremely to act right,
As witness his clear legal claim to Scotlands' throne,
Argued in court, and then afield, with weapons drawn.
To those brave chiefs whose title-deeds were lost or old
New ones were granted for some small return in gold.
Warenne's debate with the Commissioners soon was done,
He simply bared his sword, " With this my lands were won
On Senlac's field, amid the passion of its pain,
And by it what my grandsires won I will retain."

" *Early Land Tenures*,"
 By C. Staniland Wake.
  Hull Literary Club, 1885.

March 10.

EARL GOWRIE AT DUNDEE.

Grim was the war. The old house stood it well,
The centre of a fierce tumultuous swell,
Whose surges flashed bright steel, and burst to flame
As the slow musketeers took careful aim.
Spears hedged the doorways, the deep windows held,
And each wild onset's furious valour quelled.
The play of sword and spear was fierce and fast,
Each ebbing surge in fury was recast
Emergent from the powder-smoke's wide flow,
To foam and drift 'mid roar and crashing blow,
And lap the building's front with gleaming war,
That sought to flood or crumble the stout bar.
Shot answered shot; the musket's blinding ire
Pierced the white-smoke drift with red shafts of fire.
The Stuart's war-cry, Gowrie's answering shout,
Rose high above the tumult of the rout;
Until fresh bands came rushing to the spot,
And poured incessantly the musket-shot,
When Gowrie, hopeless of the burghers' aid,
Re-sheathed his sword, and proud submission made.

"*An Auld Scotch Town,*"
    By *David Maxwell,*
        Hull Literary Club, 1884.

March 11.

FAIR ROSAMOND.

We may get somewhat stiff and dry—
Throat-stretched with looking up too-high—
So now and then a story old
Is welcome, almost, as fine gold.
More welcome still if Prince or King
Makes love without the wedding ring,
In some remote old feudal age
Our love of scandal to engage,
Without the need to heave one sigh
O'er sinners so long dead and dry.
The King and Rosamond—sweet dove—
Were simply close as hand and glove,
But he was fettered with a quean,
Of reputation beyond screen ;
Wherefore he visited—oh, fie !—
His little darling on the sly—
So did his Queen with, poison cold,
And dagger, for the minx so bold !
If you don't think this story true,
Refer to Leech, his picture view !

"*The Fable of Fair Rosamond,*"
By *Thos. Walton, M.R.C.S., F.C.S., &c.*
Hull Literary Club.

March 12.

THE QUESTION.

Where does the electric impulse lie—
In pressure of a tiny hand,
Or witchcraft of a tender eye?

Was it Omphale's tender sigh
That Hercules could not withstand?—
Where does the electric impulse lie?

None may its potent art deny,
None may its subtle course command—
The witchcraft of a tender eye.

E'en Dian's cold breast made reply,
She chastest of the Heathen band!—
Where does the electric impulse lie?

And Vulcan of the swarthy dye
Met smiling Venus's demand,
The witchcraft of her tender eye.

We ask, as love and being fly
Throughout the gay idyllic land,
Pray does the electric impulse lie
In witchcraft of a tender eye?

"*Life's Electricity and the Electricity of Life,*"
By *J. Alexander, M.R.C.S.,*
Hull Literary Club, 1883.

March 13.

EDWARD IV. SHUT OUT OF HULL.

    Yes, he's landed! stormy seas
Gave our island no release;
And with banner in the gale
Tossing o'er his burnished mail,
Edward marches through the land,
With his Flemmings, gun-in-hand.
Shall we throw the strong gates wide
For the Yorkist, in his pride?—
We who marched with Hanson out
For red Sandal's stormy bout,
When Duke Richard met his doom,
In the old year's dying gloom.
In the hour that Bolingbroke
Fair but falsely to us spoke,
Did our fathers slacken chain,
Let the drawbridge fall again?
Nay! with arrow on the string,
Warned they off their future King:
And thus we, with spear and sword,
Menace back our late liege lord.

To Geo. P. Craven,
  Roland Garden,
    London.

March 14.

DAWSON, THE ARTIST.

He is beyond our pity! laid at rest,
And honoured with the guerdon of just fame,
So long delayed unto his earnest aim,
Approving him with long continued test.
Rich in his poverty, of love opprest,
And of his daily worship reaping blame
That could not quench the ardour of his flame,
Devouring of his Summer days the best.
Hard was the toil, thrice earned the artist's bread,
As genius won the wrinkles of dull care,
The thought-vext brow, the grey-besprinkled head,
But kept the inner joy, the presence fair,
The spirit's holy triumph to declare,
As eve declined, by night's deep glooms o'erspread.

"*Dawson, the Artist*,"
  By *John Potter Briscoe, F.R.H.S.*,
    Hull Literary Club, 1881,

March 15.

HOTHAM DEMANDS ADMISSION.

ATTEND my friends! for once let prudence rule
Our party aims, and yield the town its due.
We must surrender governance. 'Tis true
We have our chartered rights—yet he's a fool
Or knave (of King or Commons the poor tool),
Who hopes to keep the old when times are new,
And high prerogative falls in our view.
You sneer!—What care I for your ridicule!
I stand on my just right. This threatened town
Is no King's town; it is the nation's charge;
We cannot hold, or yield it to the crown.
Sir John must enter—let the bridges down!
The King and Commons may their claim enlarge,
'Gainst the impending storm be Parliament our targe.

"*The Mayor, Thos. Raikes, in Debate.*"
    To Samuel Davis,
            Hull.

March 16.

BOOKSELLERS' SIGNS.

Booksellers' Signs! a pleasant theme
To float us down time's rolling stream,
Through London-streets, dim, quaint, and old,
But touched with thoughts that turn to gold
The scattered relics of an age
Whose imprint gilds the historic page.
Here from this corner take the row—
A fair perspective—all aglow
With sunset's gold and crimson stain,
Flashing from sign and window-pane;
And tell me if these pictures fair
Claim not the critic's gentle care.
Draw near, and take them one by one
Ere day's red sunset gleam be done;
For they are no mere daubs, to shame
The artist's skill, their owner's name;
But drawn in such good faith and art,
The worth of knowledge to impart.
That artist's skill and author's grace,
As type and woodcut, here embrace.

"*Bookseller's Signs of London.*"
    By W. G. B. Page.
        Hull Literary Club, 1886.

March 17.

QUEEN HENRIETTA AT BRIDLINGTON.

> Warily watched grim Batten
>   Upon the wintery wave,
> A lady in laces and satin
>   Braving the sullen knave!
>
> Poor little lady! her cargo
>   Was simply steel and lead,
> With a little powder for war, so
>   Cannon you know are fed.
>
> Van Tromp, like a brick, to guide her,
>   Sailed in his stately way,
> A chivalrous sailor, beside her,
>   Into Burlington Bay!
>
> Poor little head, it was tired,
>   And well disposed for sleep,
> When Batten bore up, and fired
>   A welcome warm and deep!
>
> Van Tromp came up like a man, anon,
>   To stop the serenade,
> When Batten, withdrawing his cannon,
>   His bow politely made.

To F. R. Carter,
  Savile House,
    Potter Newton,
      Leeds.

March 18.

A MEMORIAL (E.C.H.L).

Sad day of unforgotten tears,
  Of death's untimely gain,
As we gaze backward through the years
  We thrill to sorrow's pain.

With girls and sturdy boy at knee,
  Our circle seems complete—
Our children miss no tone of glee,
  No pale face, calm and sweet.

They touch the babe's green, grassy bed,
  The roses on his tree;
They whisper of their brother dead;
  His face they never see.

We see it waxen, lily-white,
  Through dim mists of our tears;
Death-beautified unto our sight,
  Through lapse of changeful years.

Young lives, our bond of love to-day,
  Draw closer heart to heart;
The closer bond of grief's sad sway
  Doth deeper love impart.

To M. A. Lamplough,
  Hull.

March 19.

"THE DRAMA."

In wild romance, in tragic scenes, the stage
Exhibits life's vicissitude and rage!
The morning sun that pranks life's field in gold
Sets o'er the lonely grave, in death-mists cold.
Beauty's alluring spell, wealth, honour, fame,
Attract, embrace, and still defeat our aim:
We grasp the substance—when death, sorrow, time
Relax our arms, and turns to dirge the chime,
That, soft and low, rang heavenly hope on earth,
Ere slow experience laboured to its birth.
From early time the stage, with facile art
Hath laboured wit and wisdom to impart;
Though foiled by prostitution to the age,
Wit, satire, passion, with the world engage.
Great minds, unhappy lives, and sorrows deep,
Before our audience in succession sweep—
Above old graves we pause 'twixt hope and sigh,
The life reads failure, but the text is high.
Ours less to judge than sift the gold from dross,
Our wealth to cherish, and deplore their loss.

"*The Drama in England,*"
   By Sidney W. Clarke,
      Hull Literary Club, 1887.

March 20.

HOTHAM DEMANDS ADMISSION.

Proved friends! the ancient fame of this good town
Hath ever been entrusted to its sons,
And shall be, so its ancient charter runs,
But held in due dependence on the crown.
Now are we called to lay our honours down,
Supinely yield our walls and shotted guns
To those whose counsel Charles, indignant, shuns—
Shall we thus tamely crush our old renown?
'Tis Parliament's behest! We play with heads!
Aye! but no violence urge upon our souls,
Immortal sentinels, in fleshly cowls
Foredoomed to end in dissolution's shreds!
I say, when trumpet sounds, and war-drum rolls,
Men die! Choose then the right—away with craven dreads!

"*Alderman Parkins in Debate*,"
 To *James Rusby, F.R.H.S.,*
  Regents Park,
   London.

March 21.

SPRING.

Fair Spring, she comes! girt round with all her flowers,
  With glowing cheeks, and laughter-loving eyes.
A lovely maiden she! 'Mid fairest bowers,—
  There is she to be seen in loveliest guise.
But shy she was to come:—stern Winter hoar
  Delayed her; for with slow pace he onward sped,
When windy, fickle March, his reign nigh o'er,
  Called star-like Celandines from sleepy bed.

But freed at last, she hastes along her way,
  And day by day more lovely doth she seem
As April nearer to the dawn of May
  Advances. Here by this woodland's limpid stream,
'Mid scent of flowers, I lie and woo her smile,
Far from the city worldling's haunts of guile.

J. R. Tutin.

To the Rev. R. Jones,
    Sudbury,
        Suffolk.

March 22.

THE PEN.

Stylus, steel-nib, grey quill, or ancient reed,
From East or West, beneath what old world gloom
Inkstained, and laid upon the writer's tomb,
Or born of later-time's prolific seed—
Steam-wrought to meet the great world's present need—
We hold you greater than the sword and plume,
That wave and glitter o'er the battles' doom.
Rare pen that doth our hungry spirit feed,
And wrenches from life's waste of dim decay
The poet's dream, the legislator's plan—
Transmitted wisdom of each fleeting day,
To prove the immortality of man,
And yield a voice from that dim realm whose ray,
But for the pen, were lost before our day began.

"*Writing Materials, Ancient and Modern,*"
By *John Linford, F.C.S.*,
Hull Literary Club, 1886.

March 23.

A CATALOGUE OF BOOKS.

A LIST of books replete with varied charms,
With long life-labour of the true and wise,
Who saw old earth and time in fairest guise,
And heard again the clang of Grecian arms,
Loud trumpet blasts, and battle's fierce alarms.
Who sang the charms of Daphne's killing eyes,
The classic art of Strephon's dying sighs,
And all the measured fullness of love's harms,
The giant minds, that chased the night of time,
Glide like dim ghosts before our mental eye,
To wave old laurels, and old life renew ;
To chase Eve's curfew with morn's Easter chime,
And urge the clouds that veiled our clearer sky,
With the calm labour of the wise and true.

To *James Miles,*
   Trinity Street,
      Leeds.

March 24.

EPIDEMIC DISEASES.

Forced from the breezy upland to the plain,
And casting far our leafy sylvan crown,
We mix, and toil to build the dreary town.
Whereby we may security attain.
There find we many a subtle woe and pain—
Perchance in silence Plague's death-seeds are strown,
And suffering turns to frenzy 'neath death's frown,
So deep the terror of its tyrant reign.
So Hull has suffered, closed unto the world,
Grass in its streets, and each grim drawbridge raised,
With silent wharves, and flag of commerce furled,
Closed churches, the All-Father's love unpraised,
The unblessed dead in pest-pits rudely hurled—
While pitying England looked upon the scene amazed.

"Epidemic Diseases,"
  By W. Holder, M.R.C.S.
    Hull Literary Club, 1884.

March 25.

YORKSHIRE PLACE NAMES.

Soundly they sleep beneath the mists of time,
Who under sterner, stormier terms of life
Hewed their wide pathway with the axe and knife,
Whose voices drift to us in olden rhyme.
Little they thought in manhood's stormy prime,
In pauses of their fierce and trying strife,
That we, in days with peace and leisure rife,
Should love old echoes—war-note and bell-chime.
To us the Folk-names of grey eld are dear ;
They bear us far upon life's backward stream—
Its cloudland margin bright with sword and spear,
And far corn land, that takes a fiery gleam—
Thus oft the old-time spirit doth appear,
In quaint old names our villages still bear.

"*Yorkshire Place Names,*"
   By *Thomas Holderness,*
      Hull Literary Club, 1881.

March 26.

TRICHINUS SPIRILIS.

Spirilis! our insidious, wretched foe,
That cuts us prematurely off at meat,
Whereby the strength that did our foes defeat
Our foil becomes, and brings our manhood low.
Old Later-Time, with harsh unkindly blow,
Wipes our thin lips as we prepare to eat,
And warns us off, from table to retreat;
Whereat we slink away, with graceless bow.
'Twere surely kind to let us die in peace,
Strong feasters of innumerable foes,
Nor by lean famine doom our swift decrease,
With lengthened visage and low drooping jaws.
To die full fleshed, 'mid sirloin, ham, and grease,
Were just fulfilment of old Nature's faithful laws.

"Trichinus Spirilis,"
  By J. W. Fraser, M.R.C.S.,
    Hull Literary Club, 1881.

March 27.

PUBLIC OPINION.

Bound is that man in worse than iron chains
Who finds no spirit answer to his quest,
No echo to his cry for souls distrest,
Where tyranny, secure in silence, reigns.
Upon his spirit press a thousand pains,
Whose fierce convulsions are, perforce, represt;
His keen eye burns in fever for the guest
Of equal heart to cleanse dishonour's stains.
In silence heard, his passion scattered far,
The press becomes the servant of his zeal;
Ten thousand back him in his Holy War,
As type wins honour from the warriors's steel.
So hath it been—upon this fateful bar
Hath Pride declined, as Justice rose to the appeal.

"*Public Opinion,*"
  By *W. Hunt,*
    Hull Literary Club, 1882.

March 28.

HOTHAM DEMANDS ADMISSION.

To his own ruin or our overthrow
The headstrong daring of our monarch tends;
'Tis prudent, therefore, for his sake to bow,
And yield the fortress to the nation's friends.
Times such as these bring ancient honours low;
We may not waive the danger that impends—
War-surges fierce that may the land o'erflow,
Ere these dark days and this sharp trouble ends.
What needs debate! Once have we thrown our gates
Wide to the royal troops, and lost all power;
And ere the struggle, with its deepening hates,
Tends to its close, we shall, some fateful hour,
For Crown and Commons end these dull debates,
And haul the Three Crowns from each lofty tower.

"*Peregrine Pelham, M.P., in Debate,*"
   To Edward H. Garbett,
      Hull.

March 29.

CAMEOS.

DEEP-CUT thy Cameos are, in tender grace,
Of life's strong form and spirit they partake;
We love them for humanity's dear sake,
So close our strength, and weakness they embrace.
The infantile sweet freshness of this face,
The bronzèd glitter of yon human snake,
The virgin whiteness of this drifting Flake,
The cold, dead heart in yon dull Pomp, we trace —
All win our tender homage to thy art!
Gross, subtle friars, caught atrip at night,
Weird Gypsies who can nature's life impart,
Brave knights, whose true swords justify in fight,
Old Classic, Pagan Bishops 'neath Death's dart,
With many forms heroic charm our sight.

"Cameos from Browning,"
  By the Rev. H. W. Perris,
    Hull Literary Club, 1886.

March 30.

HISTORY AND POETRY.

The field is set, and the monarch's shield
    Sets all the van ablaze!
The war begins, and the brave knights wield
Falchion and lance 'till the storm-strewn field
    Reddens in sunset-rays!
'Twas nobly fought in the cause of right—
Fair day! thy laurel shall know no night.

Old men grow weary, their winter cold
    Glooms to its frozen night!
They tell the tale of their war-path bold,
Their Winter is touched by Summer's gold
    To July's sunny light!
The monk with his pen writes down the deed,
That the centuries yet to come may read.

The poet reads, and his heart throbs fast
    Old glories to rehearse!
The light of his living mind is cast
On dust and ashes of ages past—
    The old fame lives in verse!
The truth was never more true than now
In right of its wide poetic flow.

"History and Poetry,"
    By S. Harris,
       Hull Literary Club, 1885.

March 31.

A TOUR IN NORWAY.

It was a time to dwell upon in after years,
When through the maze of time, its laughter and its tears,
We turn to our forsaken youth, and conjure forth
From its dim realm the treasure of its purer worth!—
How laughter brimmed our hearts! The rock and roll of wave
Its tribute claimed—and, true physician, virtue gave!
By steam and surge across the wide sea quickly borne
We skirted Norway's craggy hem one rain-dimmed morn.
Thenceforth the all too swift, but rarely happy days
Passed like a tranquil dream—and now a Summer's maze
Of rock and stream, wild waterfalls, and lofty trees
Blend with indented cliffs, deep fiords, and rolling seas—
The stern magnificence of Nature's wilder mould
Blue canopied, and in soft regal sunshine rolled!—
You see that radius? A Norseman's strong right arm
Once nourished it with life-blood, flowing strong and warm,
And great broad bands of muscle gave it nervous power
When raged the storm in war or heaven's tempestuous hour.
It is an old ancestral relic, and whene'er
I gaze upon it, the Norse hero's land grows near!

"*A Tour in Norway*,"
    By *C. H. Milburn, M.B.,*
        Hull Literary Club.

APRIL.

Treasures of tenderness in thy blue eyes
The hidden grace of womanhood bespeak,
Veiled in the joyousness, so shy and meek,
That love shall startle with its glad surprise.
Blue are the changeful, happy April skies,
Wooing the landscape, late so cold and bleak,
Or drenching with soft showers, in frolic freak,
The meadow's verdure and faint floral dyes.
All nature wakes to smile and low birth-song,
Flushed in sweet incense of the budding flowers,
Whose wealth sets all the gay, green earth abloom.
Oh, happy life and earth! to which belong
Fair hope and sunshine of those fertile hours,
With insect-hum, and flashing of bird plume.

To Geo. Markham Tweddell,
    Stokesley.

April 1.

THE MASSACRE AT YORK, A.D., 1190.

BLEAK winds of March sweep with wild shriek and sigh
O'er ancient York, resting beneath dull night,
So dark and cheerless, save where cressets bright
Gleam from the walls and Clifford's ramparts high—
Red tongues of Hell against a starless sky !
Well might the stars refuse their purer light,
Long doomed to witness many an awful sight
From their black setting in earth's canopy.
The brute-roar of the mob swells high and far,
Red torches flare along the city ways ;
The axes beat and hew as shrieks arise—
Death-plaints that answer to the murderer's war—
And the Jews' quarter bursts into a blaze
That crimsons the vast darkness of the skies.

To Samuel Waddington,
   London.

April 2.

THE FATE OF LORD CLIFFORD.

There had been heavy blows, and in the snow
The blood glowed with a deep, accusing red
Against the waxen features of the dead,
Torn, beaten, by deep stab or heavy blow:
Clifford spurred hard, hot wrath upon his brow,
For well had Falconberg's fierce charges sped,
And poured defeat upon his haughty head,
His blood-fraught, hard earned laurels bringing low.
'Twas but a skirmish ere the battle burst,
And Clifford's heart beat proudly at the thought,
As, reining in, beside a quiet brook,
He raised the cup to quench his burning thirst;
When, lo! a headless arrow swift death brought,
And battle hopes his labouring breast forsook.

Dr. G. H. Crowther, M.S.A., &c., &c.
  St. John's, Wakefield.

April 3.

THE CELL ON THE MOOR.

A LONE, low moor, stretched underneath a sky
That frowns upon it, cold with clouds and awe;
Sparse, nakéd bushes shiver to and fro,
Where blighting winds, with low, sad moanings fly.
Here bones of unremembered travellers lie,
Murdered, or doomed to die in midnight woe:
Grim wolves, or more abhorréd human foe,
Stern-hearted, law or pity to defy,
Here prowl, to seize and rend their helpless prey,
When the short day dies in the arms of night.
Yet, in this scene, so desolate and dread,
Two holy fathers make their home, to pray
For souls, to guide the travellers aright,
And from storm, wolf, and felon shield his head.

To Geo. Bohn,
    Tranby Park, Hessle.

April 4.

FRIENDSHIP.

Some friendships live amid life's strain and fret
Unchanged, nay, strengthened by the troubled years;
And they who mingled youthful hopes and fears,
Shall clasp the hands, grown wrinkled since they met
In boyhood's days; and will, 'ere suns shall set,
Recount the glory, tragedy, and tears
That filled their days: and shall, as disappears
The last, renew their vows—Shall we forget
The past? Not so, dear friend! I hear the call
Of vanished years; their music fills my dreams,
And oft my heart goes out to thee, for all
The years come back. As lads the morning beams
Spoke of our troth. O may, as shadows fall,
Our hands be clasped beneath the sun's last gleams!

F. L. Shillito.

To an Old Friend (E L.)

April 5.

GERMANY'S STRUGGLE FOR UNITY.

Sad is the chapter of Germania's woe,
Yet claiming tribute of her later fame,
When, casting off her weakness and her blame,
In arms she met and triumphed o'er her foe.
The backward glance, all pitiful, with awe
Beholds red Jena, Auerstadt's vanquished aim ;
Crushed, shattered legions, whom no strength could tame,
Wide plains, enwrapped in devastation's flow.
From ruin see a nation, armed, arise ;
From poet-souls its war-notes hurl afar ;
Its hundred banners billowing to the skies,
And all its soul enkindled to the war.
Through death-vexed storms the bleeding eagle flies ;
The clouds disperse, and shines serene the nation's star,

"*Germany's Struggle for Unity,*"
By G. Krause, P.H., D.
Hull Literary Club, 1887.

Dr. Krause served as Fahnrich, or sub-lieutenant, of the 77th Infantry during the Franco-Prussian war, and was decorated with the Iron Cross.

April 6.

A SPIRIT-WREATH.

Weaving sweet memories, life's diviner blooms,
   To form a spirit-wreath on this sad day,
   Unfading tribute that our spirits pay,
As olden breezes, burthened with perfumes,
Sigh softly 'mid the silence of the tombs,
   We bury not our love, but meekly lay
   Our wreathéd memories, that shall ne'er decay,
Above the silent grave, to chase its glooms.

The tender service of thy many years
   In gentle thoughts unto our hearts return;
   The fires of home upon its hearthstone burn,
Seen in the twilight through a mist of tears.
No more our heavy grief, despondent fears,
   Hope-ashes that we strove in vain to urn,
   Thy tender love shall fearfully discern—
But, Oh! how deeply its lost grace endears.

To the Memory of my Mother.

April 7.

SPRING FRESCOES.

The falling of cold, fertile rain
On springing grass of tender stain.

The flow of water clear and cold,
Life-odours from the moist brown mould.

A spray of moss, a blade of grass,
Dim shadows as the grey clouds pass.

A daisy white, with golden eye;
Bird-twitter where the brown wings fly.

A sudden joy, a burst of bloom,
A world of light and mild perfume.

Green grass and leaves—abundant birth—
Great hope and promise in the earth.

Laburnum and pale lilac stain;
The brown earth clad in springing grain.

A sweet child in a snowy bed,
Buds wreathed about its golden head.

To Dr. C. F. Forshaw, F.R.M.S., F.G.S.,
  Bradford, Yorks.

April 8.

ALL SAINTS', DRIFFIELD.

In olden days of warlike throes
Unto the Lord this church arose;
Built, it may be, by mailëd hands
Not slow in flashing of red brands:
Rough hands, to score each guilty stain
Deep in the heart's dull yearning pain.
Seeking the Lord, their sins to heal,
The builders wrought with holy zeal,
And o'er the relics of a ruder day
God's house arose from its decay.

Their crests are low, their banners rent,
Their arms beneath the battlement
Brave the rude elements to-day—
Texts of mutation and decay;
But, in the Father's hand possesst,
Faith views each ransomed soul at rest,
Hearing where battle-cries arose
The healing wisdom of God's laws,
And where the sinner lost his care
Far echoes of sweet praise and prayer.

To the Rev. Canon Newton, M.A.,
 Driffield.

April 9.

THE PAPAL INTERDICT: HIGH CHURCH CLOSED.

Dumb, death-stricken, lies the church,
   With barred, forbidding door;
Slowly 'neath its reverend porch
   The burghers pass no more!
Is faith dead in a Pagan land,
Or what grim tyrant sways command?

Comes no tone of Jesus' voice
   To call our children home;
No fair bride doth here rejoice,
   Moving beneath God's dome!
Hath childhood fair, hath love's embrace,
Drifted beyond the Father's grace?

Dim bereavement gathers here
   No message sweet from Nain;
Finds the sinner in his fear
   No solace for his pain!
Unblesséd are the sleeping dead,
No light of heaven to guilt is shed!

A drifting echo from proud Rome
Sealed to our need the heavenly dome.

To the Rev. Canon McCormick,
   Hull.

April 10.

DAY DREAMS AT HOWDEN.

Slow o'er the surface of the broad, calm stream
We drift, and weave in light our golden dream,
Hearing thy bells through centuries sweetly chime
In happy pauses of this tranquil time!

The Barons pass, with sword and lance
Wreathed with the Fleur-de-lis of France;
Or seek far Calvary's mount of pain,
Beneath the cross of ruddy stain!
Page, jongleur, squire, and portly priest
One moment throng to prayer and feast,
Then Howden feels the Tudor's hand
Outstretched in ruinous command;
And follows fast the wild war-peal,
The terror of the Roundheads' steel;
Then joy-bells shake the leaves of May,
Flaunts Charles o'er Cromwell's dim decay!

Fair dreams with day depart—'tis evensong,
So dust and time o'erhap life's right and wrong,
And in the twilight's dim religious calm
After hot sun and dream, falls sweeter balm!

To the Rev. W. Hutchinson, M..1.,
   The Vicarage,
      Howden.

April 11.

FOREST LEAVES.

Forest leaves unfold to fade
In the woodland's sunny glade;
Born in weakness, storm and tear,
In Autumn-gusts they disappear.
Frail as the leaf, in weakness born,
How soon man from the earth is torn!
So frail his record on the soil,
So dim the laurels of his toil!
The honours of his shield decay,
As sunset bounds his fleeting day.

Forest lays! the sweet bird-song
Doth our Summer joy prolong;
But no music sweet and clear
Doth charm the death-gusts of the year.
Now memory makes the green wood ring
With wild war-shout and twanging string,
And brings the old life back again,
With flashing spears and banner's stain;
Where echoes of the woods embrace
The axe's stroke and hurrying chase.

"*Lays and Leaves of the Forest of Knaresborough,*"
   By the Rev. Thos. Parkinson, F.R.H.S.,
     Northallerton.

April 12.

THE FIGHT AT SELBY, A.D. 1643.

Softly the April sun shone down
On the red-tiled roofs of Selby town,
Where many a gallant Cavalier
Rent the air with a loyal cheer,
Meeting the charge that Fairfax made,
When storming trench and barricade,
With pistol, halberd, sword and pike,
Quick to parry and keen to strike,
Filling the balmy air of Spring
With the loyal cry, " God save the King."

Strong entrenchment and barricade
Failed to stop the Roundhead raid;
Over the debris, over the dead,
The gallant chargers swiftly sped
Into the mélée's deadly strife;
Into the struggle of death and life,
Scattering left and scattering right
The Cavaliers in hurried flight;
Shaking King Charles's royal crown
In the gallant fight at Selby town.

To John H. Wurtzburg, D. D. LAMPLOUGH.
  Armley Road,
    Leeds.

April 13.

NEWS FROM SELBY.

Forth they went, horse and foot, proud and strong,
To the righting of the nation's wrong:
But a handful; banners drifting,
Harness gleaming, and each heart lifting
Prayer for light and guidance from the Lord,
Giving point and sharpness to the sword.
How we followed them with wistful heart,
Praying God to prove their righteous part!

Southward, King and Commons were at play,
Vainly wrestling for the victor's bay!
Northward, Leslie and his Scots held close
By Newcastle's strong Northumbrian force!
Saving Hull alone, the broad shire lay
Armed and loyal to King Charles's sway.

Selby, trenched and strong, the first grim bar,
Stayed the drifting surges of our war;
When, with clash of pike and wild sword-play,
Muskets booming, blurred we that fair day!
In the wild war-drift of smoke and flame
Won we Selby—first mark of our aim.

To C. H. Marriott, J.P.,
  Manor Lawn,
    Dewsbury.

April 14.

YORKSHIRE SCENES.

STORMY clangour, mortal foes
Wrestling in their red death-throes,
Underneath the storm-curst skies,
Where the Roman eagles rise.

*Through such agonies of birth
Rise the Nations of the earth.*

Smitten by the Saxon steel
Pict and Scot in ruin reel;
And King Arthur, whirling by,
Casts Excalibur on high.

*Demigods must tread the earth
'Ere a Nation bleeds to birth.*

Smoke and blood and fiery stain
Paints the passion of the Dane,
'Ere the Norman's iron hand
Curbs with walls the mighty land.

*Relics of a Nation's birth,
Shattered chains bestrew the earth.*

" *Old Yorkshire,*"
   By William Smith, F.S.A.S.,
     Morley.

April 15.

IN THE CITY.

With his great heart, pitiful and strong,
Bursts the new-world poet into song!
He who loves the greenwood still and wild,
Hears the plaintive weeping of a child;
Weeping, dying, in the city grim,
Poisoned by the foul air, thick and dim;
Fading like a wild flower torn away
From green meadows where the sunbeams play.

Then responds the poet to the child,
From his maze of fairy dreams beguiled,
Holds to earth the dead form, wan and thin,
Points the gilded city to its sin:
So holds the pale babe in the sunshine,
In the glory of its light divine,
That the cruel wrong wrought to the dead
Shall far o'er the broad, wide earth be spread!

For the poet's mission is to tell
The old, common crimes that spring from hell,
And so wring the heart to life and shame
That it answers to the teacher's claim.

"*City Ballads*,"
    By Will Carleton.

Will Carleton was the guest of the Hull Literary Club at their Annual Dinner, October 8th, 1884.

April 16.

THE OLD HOME-ROAD.

'Tis wise old travel-memories to retain,
Be the scene distant, or the old home-road
Through fertile Yorkshire to our heart-abode,
By pleasant meadows and broad fields of grain.
With pensive joy through years of fret and stain
We scan the path, and fain would cast our load
Aside—Cares burthen that will still corrode,
Until reluctant feet our last stage gain.
Pride, sin, may come between us and our God,
Yet have we rendered unaffected love,
In that our lips have touched earth's fair green sod—
Our Nature's homage to the Lord above,
Through His great system, all too weakly trod;
Yet of such adoration wilt Thou not approve?

"*A Topographical Tour,*"
    By G. H. Lennard,
        Hull Literary Club, 1880.

April 17.

REVOLT.

The tyrannies of these late times sit ill
    Upon the people's neck, who, keen-eyed, see
    Europe's convulsive wrestling to be free
From lesser evils, curbing their proud will.
Yet, seeing this, what use our " Peace be still!"
    The chain that binds is their revolt's decree;
    The straitest held most need their liberty,
In closest strait exerting greatest skill.
    Why preach? a common value edges life—
O'er-run its grounds, the common value falls;
    All men are equal in resultant strife:
The oppressed unto the oppressor calls,
    Points to his troubled day, with sorrow rife,
And, barred the open strife, to murder crawls.

"*The Czar and His Subjects,*"
    By R. S. *Pickering,*
        Hull Literary Club, 1880.

April 18.

THROUGH NATURE

Oh earth! our idol worship, pure and dim,
Of bird or flower, broad plain or mountain high,
Robbed not the Spirit of the shrouding sky
Of one soul-prayer, or praise-pervaded hymn!
Since thirsty lips have touched the goblet's brim
Low music mingles with each yearning sigh,
And hope supernal, that shall never die,
Though death's cold palsy smites each fettered limb.
It is one unity of sky and earth,
One holy Lord who reigns supreme above!
And we, who kneel in adoration deep,
And tremble through long sorrow to our birth,
Responsive to one unity of love,
The holier homage to our Maker keep.

To Claude Leatham,
  The Red House,
    Wentbridge, Pontefract.

April 19.

SANCTUARY AT BEVERLEY.

Way for the red-handed slayer of man!
Way through the terror and tempest of night—
Clouds of grim blackness are torn by the light—
Way for the fugitive under death's ban.
Wave the keen sword and the sharp partisan,
Brandished by strong hands the slayer to smite—
Way for him, reeling and dizzy in flight,
Close on his tracks the pursuer's fierce van!
Open the gates! he is saved from his doom—
Leave him to sob in his passion for breath,
Wiping red stains from his guilty right-hand!
Silent his victim, arrayed for the tomb—
Pale women and children wailing his death,
Yesterday standing a lord in the land!

To the Rev. H. E. Nolloth, B.D.,
  The Minster Vicarage,
    Beverley.

April 20.

THE FIELD OF TOWTON.

In Saxton Church the peasants met,
    The holy mass to hear;
On Towton field the war was set
    With banner and bright spear!
The earth was white with frozen snow
The sky hung dark and low—
Proud man commingled spear and palm
On God's high day of peace and calm.

The trumpets rang, the arrows flew,
    A drifting gale of death;
The fiercely swirling tempest blew
    The banners on its breath.
Upon the trampled snow were spread
The cold forms of the dead!
The blast was charged with missile rain
That smote, to spread war's dreadful stain.

And all the day, 'mid clangour wild,
    War-column's flow and drift,
The field of Towton was defiled
    By the keen falchion's thrift.

To John R. Cordingley,
    Bradford.

April 21.

A BOOK OF POEMS.

He is a benefactor great
Who holds the poet's high estate ;
   The burthen of his smiles and tears,
With breathings of most gracious art
He doth unto our soul impart,
   And sicknesses' long sorrow cheers.

This little book is full of thought,
Into melodious measure wrought ;
   And in my father's last sad pain
The wisdom of each gifted page
Would many a pleasant hour engage,
   Won from his suffering's reign.

In thought I see his manly face,
The pleasant little garden space,
   Cool shadiness of lilac leaves,
Geraniums glowing at his feet,
Resting from toil and wild sea-beat,
   In the last calm that Autumn weaves.

'Twas long for suffering, short for love,
Ere God's full mercy he did prove.

To my Sister Ellinor.

April 22.

THEN AND NOW.

The life-draught bubbles to the silver rim,
Flower-petals quiver in the Summer sheen;
Nought under God's blue sky is base or mean!
The future—Fairy-land! veiled, sweetly dim.
Behold bright mail, wild Orson's brawny limb,
Pathfinder, Uncas, and meek Verdant Green!
Arabian Nights drift star-glow o'er the scene,
Where Janus-Fiction's smile grows dark and grim.
My mirth's low laughter echoes through the years,
Old features lighten to their early grace;
Through a far drifting maze of care and fears
I see, in sweet serenity, truth's face!
Old eyes grow dim; the death-toll smites my ears;
Old friends fall off; I near the last goal of the race!

To the Rev. E. Bradley,
   (Cuthbert Bede),
      Lenton Vicarage,
         Grantham.

April 23.

CHARLES I. AT HULL.

Unhappy Charles! why did not April gloom
To mid December, and fair morn to night,
As thou pursued the pathway of thy might,
Nor dreampt it lead unto a tragic doom?
'Twas but the prelude to the strife—the boom
Of cannon, and the musket's fierce red light,
Succeeded, as the falchion, flashing bright,
Laid in red swaithes the harvest of the tomb.
Sad was the day, when at the gates of Hull
The loud notes of thy trumpets rang in vain,
Grim cannon frowning in thy royal face,
As Hotham, in stern zeal undutiful,
Dared the old town against its King maintain,
And scorned the pledges of thy royal grace.

To the Rev. J. L. Saywell, F.R.H.S.,
    (Yorkshire Historian).

April 24.

THE DUKE OF YORK AT HULL.

Charles was at York! the war was drawing near,
And Hotham held old Hull with jealous fear.
Day-long tried troops were on the guard—at night
The gates were barred—red cressets gave their light.
With jar and jangle peace was set adrift—
Some waited but the sign bright swords to lift.
One April day young York set state aside
And sought the town, to view its bulwarked pride.
Brave men were with him in the market throng:
Well known were they—their presence might mean wrong!
Soon came the mayor—heart-veiled, in courteous guise—
To show the prince high honour, and devise
Banquet and feast, those pageantries of state
Which veil so oft the midnight of our hate!
So all went well. Night sped, and dawned the day—
King Charles was at the gate in proud array,
To find the bridges raised, the cannon out,
Armed Hull prefiguring the nation's doubt.
Later, day drawing on its veil of grey,
Came York, with his rejected sire to spur away.

To F. W. Pattison,
    Burwood Place,
        London, W.

April 25.

THE HERALD AT THE GATE.

Men speak low in their homes to-night,
   And women's prayers are deep and long :
Now are we bound to dare the fight ;
The sword shall arbitrate our manhood's right,
   And Charles requite our wrong.
If England's righteous blood be foully shed,
The guilt be on his head.

We have not wrought to slay, and steep
   The green sod in a rain of gore !
The harvest we would gladly reap
Is right and truth—not battle's mangled heap,
   With woman's tears shed o'er !
We fear not, but we grieve to draw the sword—
Defend the guiltless, Lord !

This morn the herald at our gate
   Pealed his loud summons for the King,
Holding the threat of traitor's fate
As meet reguerdon of our rebel hate,
   Should our presumption wring
From mercy's mood to wrath the monarch's heart—
He bootless did depart !

To Alfred Denniss,
    Hull.

April 26.

A MEMORIAL.

The angels would not let thee tread earth's throng
Of fretting cares. Thy feet were never stained
By mire or clay; nor was thy spirit pained
By cross or spear. Two years! The time seemed long
To them :—and now thy stainless feet among
The flowers of Eden tread, and Heaven has gained,
But ours the bitter loss. Our Summer waned
When thou didst pass—our sunlight and our song !—
O Edie! child of love—our hearts are sore,
And time heals not! We call by day and night
For thee, and wait, and lift up evermore
To Heaven our piercèd hands. There all is light!
And thou art there! Enough!—Keep near the door,
Reveal thy glory to our tear-dimmed sight!

F. L. Shillito.

To Edie,
   In Sunny Paradise.

April 27.

THE LEGEND OF WATTON ABBEY.

Poor lady, in that leaguered hold distresst,
'Mid fierce alarm, wild storm, loud trumpet peal,
And midnight dreams of red impending steel,
Her comfort was the sweet babe at her breast;
Her hope, that some fair day her husband's crest
Should top the surges of the battle reel,
His gentle care her lengthened sorrows heal—
Her drooping beauty in his arms impresst.
It might not be—her wealth of jewels won
Her quick despatch from all the ills of time.
In midnight storm the dreadful deed was done,
And morn stole softly on the scene of crime,
Lit by the tender sorrow of the sun,
While rolled the solemn requiem from the distant gun.

To James Lister,
   Rockwood House,
     Ilkley.

April 28.

A REMONSTRANCE FROM HULL, A.D., 1642.

  Bend, Charles, thy monarch's will before the sum
    Of England's strength, on Freedom all-intent ;
  Strike ill advice and low ambition dumb,
    And heal, by kingly grace, the woeful rent
    Which severs hearts, and feeds sharp discontent !
  Thy sons are free ! Vain note of trump and drum,
    With clangour fierce of arms and armour blent,
  To awe one British heart, its courage numb,
    And hurl its hopes down ruin's swift descent.
  Start back !—The shadow of impending years
    O'erglooms the terrors of thy helmèd brow,
  Its dim, dense veil involving blood and tears
    Which thy ambition's crime may cause to flow.
  We tremble not—nor thou ! Life's craven fears
    Smite not our strength, nor bring thy purpose low.

To W. Hill,
    Hull.

April 29.

EASINGTON, HOLDERNESS.

There is an old tradition that the King,
Grave Charles, that prince of melancholy mien,
In the first days of warfare sought this scene,
So tranquil in the balm and grace of Spring,
So far removed from faction's bitter sting,
And passed one night in slumber most serene—
The loyal roof of Overton his screen,
Who was so soon to hear the trumpets ring,
And face his foemen on the marshalled plain,
Beneath the banner of the threatened crown,
A crimson drift above the night of war!
No credence may this olden legend gain,
Yet here the King might well lay trouble down
In sleep, 'ere banners gathered from afar.

To John Ombler,
   Kilnsea,
      Holderness

April 30.

MISS BRADDON'S "BARBARA."

Ah, Barbara! as the white rose pure and sweet,
So maidenly and true; with clinging heart
Strained to the breaking, with dear hopes to part,
We follow the sad pathway of thy feet
Where oft thy soldier-lover thou didst meet,
In all shy loyalty above the art
Whereby the coquette feathers Cupid's dart,
To wail her folly's guerdon in defeat.
Her heaven she buries in the parent earth,
Where lily-bells shed fragrance in the Spring,
Then, wan and pale, a bruisèd dove, she flits
From grave to bridal, smiling hope to dearth
So desolate, nor bud nor swallow's wing
One promise of sweet bloom or song admits.

To Miss Louise Elliott,
  The Hollies,
    Nutley.

MAY.

Oh, Nature's Princess! in the path of May,
    The sweetest bud of all the garden's bloom,
Straying amid its tincture and perfume,
    With smiles that answer to the happy day.
All thoughts divine thy spirit doth obey,
    Swift as the light gleam of an angel's plume,
Cleaving the shadow of our lower gloom
    At God's behest, with one brief, heavenly ray!
Thy white robe flits amid the springing flowers,
    Birds melt in song about thy happy way,
White daisies fringe the pathway of thy feet,
    And love is lurking round thy scented bowers.
Oh, sunny skies! that seldom gloom to grey,
    Gild the green May-time of this maiden sweet.

To Mrs. Susan K. Phillips,
    Greenroyd, Ripon.

May 1.

IN LOVE AND GRIEF.

My dear old friend, I'll note to-day
  One sorrow of the few we note,
As o'er the old foot-trodden way
  Our pilgrim-toil is dumbly wrought—
The May-day Sabbath woke my fear;
  My little daughter, pale and sad,
Too brave to shed a single tear,
  Must leave her home, and blanket-clad,
Be carried to the fever-home,
  "For life or death"—so beat the rhyme
In heart and brain! Nor would it roam,
  But wrought in dull and rhythmic time.
Poor babe! racked heart and brain that wrought—
  The jar and clangour of the bell
Smote my dull ear; the postman brought
  A small white card, known but too well,
And in it with dim eyes I read
  Death's message, thy bereavement sad;
Then bowed, with added grief, my head,
  And yet to touch thy soul was glad.

To the Rev. F. L. Shillito,
  Blackburn.

FRESCOES.

May 2.

ALDERMAN WILLIAM GEE.

DIMLY through the mists of changing time,
With its old-world storm of wrath and crime,
Looms before us this old merchant prince,
True and generous—as his deeds evince.

He was of the brave old Tudor age,
Stiff and stately, with its gusts of rage,
Fuming out in passion fierce and hot,
Wild war-scenes with Spanish Don, or Scot;

Or a clutch at that old demon's beard,
Harry, for state-murders cursed and feared—
A mean lot, those Tudors, vain and proud,
Sorry upstarts of the kingly crowd !

In such troublous times of storm and roar
Lofty honours our old townsman bore—
Twice Sheriff, thrice Mayor, with good heart
His great wealth and talent to impart.

To rebuild the Grammar School his gold
Went freely, also to house the old,
'Ere, full of years, his life's labour sped
Bowed he to death's rest his sage old head.

To James Brodie Hickman,
    Hull.

May 3.

THE DRAMA.

BETTER our tears for mimic woes should fall,
   Our honest tribute to the actor's art,
Than we should hold, dry-eyed, our cynic part,
   Until life's curtain falls—without recall.
Yet has life woe and mirth enough for all,
   Full exercise for gentle, loving heart,
For tender hands to soothe its throbbing smart,
   For honest service, beauty to enthral.
Nay, faithful art, that breathes its passion clear,
   And stands before us in its sentient life,
Its laurel all undimmed by blood or tear,
   Should gain some plaudit from our painful strife;
While our demand approved our spirit's gain,
   And cleansed high art from sin's defiling stain.

"*The Drama.*"
  By Hy. Rose,
    Hull Literary Club, May 3rd, 1880.

May 4.

AURORA AND THE SUN-GOD.

Clouds bar the green earth from his straining eyes;
   The golden-gates of morn his shackles are,
   He throbs to see the pale stars fade afar,
As the first blushes of Aurora rise:
Eastward her glory floods the trembling skies;
   She drifts and lingers o'er each burning bar,
   Driving the black cloud-curtains with her car,
Until the golden gate wide open flies.
The rose tints of her robe one moment shade
   The burning glory of his gracious face,
Then, like another Semele, her charms
Into the burning godhead meekly fade,
   Lost in the fervour of his hot embrace,
As the responsive earth to life and passion warms.

To J. R. Tutin,
    Hull.

May 5.

HOW PRINCE OLAVE SAILED DOWN THE HUMBER.

Sullen and dark each brow,
As we pointed the crested prow
Downward against the river's flow,
    And strained at the bending oar!

Along the vessel's side
The rush of the flowing tide
Roared as in scorn at our subdued pride,
    As its adverse course it bore;

And the charnel shore as we passed
Tainted the east-winds chilly blast
    That sullen against us tore,
    With its angry rush and roar.

Oh! how we cursed the day
That we sailed from Norroway
With our raven-banners fluttering gay,
    And sails to the North-wind spread.

Kingless and conquered now,
With our bravest buried low,
Shame and despair dwell upon each brow,
    As we mourn for the mighty dead.

                                          D. D. Lamplough.

To J. A. Duesbury,
    Postmaster,
        Hull Literary Club.

May 6.

THE SPANISH INVASION.

Shall we be slack to meet the Don,
Who boast green laurels largely won
At Agincourt and Poitiers,
When France was bathed in blood and tears?
Stained laurels! Yet they proved the men,
And stout are we as our sires then;
Nor flinch to meet with pike and sword
Spanish cut-throat—spearman or lord!
We dare to claim Heaven's strength and aid
To point our halberd, edge our blade;
And come the Spaniard when he may
We'll grip his throat in mortal fray.
Yes! to the war we stand enrolled,
Offer our lives and hard-earned gold:
We'll do our part to fit for sea
The fleet that keeps our honour free,
And save our brave land from the stain
Of inroad by the hordes of Spain;
Not, by our manhood and God's grace,
That we fear to meet them face to face.

To Charles A. Federer, L.C.P.,
 Bradford.

May 7.

THE NUMISMATIST.

Coins are my books!—Romance and art,
Love and war, Mars' sword, Cupid's dart,
Iscariot's passion, Timon's cave,
Midas' grief, Danae's golden wave,
Speak in the circle of this gold
Whose coiners rest in Hades' fold.
Coins are the worldling's golden sun,
Round which his narrow life is spun.
I, you see, take it otherwise,
Fix on these coins a higher prize—
The sum of Grecian strength and grace
Behold in this Jove-stricken face;
This broad-piece speaks of Charles's reign,
This gold doubloon of Philip's Spain.
An evil glamour you may see
Stamped in each ancient deity;
For these cold discs were potent gods,
Smiting the earth with swords and rods,
And trampling under blood-wet feet
The ebbing surges of retreat.

To Councillor C. E. Fewster,
   Hull Literary Club.

May 8.

LOANS FOR CHARLES I.

Our generous hand had yielded gold
    Profusely to the King—
Our love his honour would enfold
    With adamantine ring!
Yet bootless was our willing aid
By fresh demands alone repaid,
    While passion shook the land;
And darker gloomed each passing year
With shadow of impending fear,
    That we could not withstand.

Grim plague had brought our fortunes low,
    And scourged us to the death;
Then came revolt's dark overflow,
    'Ere we could gather breath.
As friends ill-used, but loving still,
We sadly strove to meet his will,
    But saw with doubt and gloom,
The ebb and turning of the tide,
The loss of loyalty's high pride,
    Presaging Charles's doom!

To *Jesse Malcolm*,
    Hull.

May 9.

THE MAYOR AND THE ARCHBISHOP.

A GILDED mace, as you may see—
A toy for gala day and glee !
Ah, well, perhaps ! but I opine
This mace would match that sword of thine.
I've seen a frailer club—a staff,
Or crosier—write an epitaph,
Or neatly score a priestly crown
As the poor father flopped him down.
The old dispute of tasting wine
Once made our bluff old Mayor shine !
The proud Archbishop and his folk
Thought to beguile him by mere talk ;
But I, who better knew his mood,
Watched with delight his mantling blood,
Until in sudden heat he tore
The staff from the poor monk who bore
The bauble, and then striking out,
Put the sad priests to woful rout—
Of course we lent some timely aid—
And in due course submission made.

To Robert Leslie Armstrong,
      Wood View, Shipley.

May 10.

THE VICAR OF CAVE'S PENANCE.

What's wrong, my friend? that you thus crowd
To sound of bell-stroke, slow, but loud,
Around this fine old church of yours,
That o'er red tile and gable towers.
A penance, eh! Cave's vicar old
Has been dispensing German gold,
Not the old coin, deep struck at Rome,
And issued from St. Peter's dome.
Ah! here he comes, head bending low,
As one who owns a shameful blow.
His grey head and thin feet are bare—
The priests are droning out a prayer.
How meek he stands, with hands across,
Yet self-possessed, and at no loss;
Stripped to his shirt; the greater shame
To—well, the source of all this blame!
He takes his faggot, marches round
The ancient building's noble bound—
'Twill be repeated!—Thank you, no!
Not thus I'd twice regard my foe.

To *T. W. Clarke*,
    Hull Literary Club.

May 11.

HULL SHIPPING OF THE PAST.

Dark were the times and frought the stormy sea
With perils great and manifold, to thwart
The mariner's brave toil and skilful art,
Who oft before the corsair turned to flee:
Yet bold the merchant, winning golden fee
For merchandise brought safely to the mart,
Nor slow his wealth in bounty to impart,
Responsive to the Church, to want's low plea.
War seized his ships, and turned his gain to loss,
At Sluys our galley sank beneath the wave;
Goods were unshipped in haste upon the quay,
And the proud galley must the channel cross,
And bear to France fierce wielders of the glaive,
To reap red fields, and spread war's tyranny.

"*Hull Shipping of the Past*,"
  By *J. Suddaby*,
    Re *The Hull and East Riding Portfolio*, *June*, 1887.

May 12.

HOME FROM SEA.

How little thought you, in your life's young day,
  With your old Norse love of the stormy sea,
  Its healthful gales and billows rolling free,
The sadness that would one late voyage repay,
When victor Death stole three sweet babes away.
  In four brief days! Dear babes, whom thou shalt see
  When all fair things of earth come back to thee,
In that far land that lies beyond decay.
  For 'tis one life, with but a grave between,
To hold the wonderous dust we need no more,
  And keep us separate from the realm unseen
Until our lost estate God shall restore!
  Wherefore we, bending o'er the grave's soft green,
In comfort, sadly sigh, " Our babes have gone before !"

To *W'm. Lamplough,*
        Hull.

May 13.

THE MINISTRY OF FLOWERS.

Ah, flowers! so fair, and sweet, and pure,
   Whose beauty makes our spirit glad!
Your short-lived charms may not endure,
But nurtured of warm sun and shower,
Ye glorify a summer's hour,
   In regal beauty clad!
How shall we own your gentle sway,
The treasure of your grace repay,
That soothes depression's moments sad,
   And suns to Summer add?

Christ's words have touched your silent grace,
   Expositors of God's high lore!
You wreathe fair childhood's happy face,
We yield our dead to your embrace;
With pensive souls your fading trace
   When Summer brief is o'er!
God's dust to dust!—we own one birth,
And fade into one common earth;
But trust God's Summer shall restore
   Your ministry once more!

"*The Ministry of Flowers,*"
  By the Rev. *Hilderic Friend*, F.L.S.

May 14.

HISTORIC YORKSHIRE.

Fair Romance! thy sunny beam
Gilds the surface of time's stream.
Though the mists of ages past
O'er its flashing waves be cast.
Abbey's arch and turret grey
Rise above the misty spray,
Clifford's broad flag floating far
With its challenge to the war;
'Neath the shimmer of the spears
Crested helm and plume appears!
(Twine the roses white and red,
Where at Towton blood was shed!)
Cold and still Duke Richard lies
Underneath the wintery skies.
Old York rings with clamour gay:
Ladies fair and monks in grey,
Haughty Barons, clad in arms,
Cavaliers from Marston's harms—
All the rout of ancient days
Sweeps before our dazzled gaze.

"*Historic Yorkshire*"
　By William Andrews, F.R.H.S.

May 15.

ON THE DEATH OF ALDERMAN FOUNTAIN.

In the swirl of the Autumn blast
The brown oak-leaves are earthward cast,
    Faint type of our decay!
Who through earth's tremour and rude strife
Bravely maintain our changeful life,
    'Till sunset closes day!
And as the leaf, swirled on the breeze,
We drift beneath the giant trees;
And the sound of the Autumn rain
Is the sole requiem of our pain.

Yet some are as the oaks that stand
Sentinels in the fair wood-land,
    As ages drift along!
They brave the storms that beat the earth,
Long centuries of sun and dearth,
    So proud are they, and strong!
The striker cometh, the oak must fall,
However stately, high, and tall!
But at their fall earth's sob of pain
Finds echo in our hearts again!

To Mrs. Gleadow, Hull.

May 16.

NEWS OF STRAFFORD'S DEATH.

King Pym has won at last great Strafford's head,
The splendid traitor lies in ruin—dead!
So well he bore himself, with noble art,
The victor's laurel almost decks his part.
Great mind was his, to shine in any strife—
Well the sick lion's grandeur fenced his life.
So great in ruin, he dwarfed all the rest,
And Pym showed badly in his bloody quest.
Yet was this noble Earl the people's foe,
A traitor, turning our just hope to woe;
And if this quarrel end in battle red,
Shall not far purer lives than his be shed?
How tamed is stubborn Charles by selfish fear,
To let this dark death-pageant thus appear.
Who'll dare to trust him, who draws coldly back
When Nemesis is on his servant's track?
In Strafford he surrendered all—for he
Might have wrought out his King's prosperity.
Abandoned Strafford! by late friends bayed down,
What sorrows o'er thy tragic grave be strown!

To E. Collishaw,
  Hull Literary Club.

May 17.

CHARLES FROST.

Not satisfied was he that Edward's day
Should fix the bounds of our historic thought:
His keen eye caught an epoch more remote,
Veiled in the haze that overspreads decay!
Beyond the banners of the Northern fray
The flags of commerce he beheld afloat,
And toiled until the truth, approved, was brought
From dim death-shades, his ardour to repay.
He added length of days unto the town,
Nor shook one laurel from King Edward's crown;
And now his labour dignifies his name,
To stand when wife and friends have passed the tomb,
The olive garland of his peaceful fame
Who won some relics from time's ancient gloom.

*Charles Frost, F.S.A.,
Author of " Notices Relative to the Early History of the Town and Port of Hull."*

*To Percival Frost,
        Cambridge.*

May 18.

CAPTAIN EDWARD LAKE.

Serene he sleeps who roved the stormy sea
  In the old days of war and fierce unrest,
  When British valour stood its utmost test,
And pushed proud banners to red victory!
'Mid battle-clouds he saw his foeman flee, *
  After fierce toil upon the wild sea-breast,
  Whereby his valour foiled the rover's quest,
And saved his manhood from captivity.
He trod the deck when Pierson held at bay
  His dreadful foe, and saved the Baltic fleet,
But could no more achieve on that sad day,
  When high achievement honoured sure defeat, †
Passed has the storm, its throes and battle-heat—
Peace doth the travail of our sires repay.

To Heneage Ferraby,
  Hull.

---

* Repulse of a privateer.   † Engagement with Paul Jones.

May 19.

SAER DE SUTTON'S CRIME.

Storm-beaten, after months of toil
A strange ship sighted Yorkshire soil!
Entered the Humber, anchored fast
In our wild river Hull at last.

Merchandise rich and jewels rare
Were the freight that the strange ship bare.
Saer de Sutton, bent on gain,
Blurred his scutcheon with dark red stain.

That night the strangers woke in woe,
And scarce the murderers' visage saw.
Dead men cumbered the bloody deck
In the young day's first sun-fleck.

Saer had jewels enough in store—
All looked ruddy with human gore!
Men talked, and turned aside in fear—
Saer's jewels were bought too dear.

Justice, blind, and wielding her sword,
Her hand stretched out, and shook a cord.
Wicked Saer with jewels bought
Peace for the crime so vainly wrought.

To Joseph Soulsby,
  Hull.

May 20.

OLD KILNSEA CHURCH.

This is Greenwood's work, from Poulson's book—
Kilnsea old church, 'ere the wild sea took
Cliff, church, God's acre, all, to its breast
In the ardour of its fierce unrest.
Twenty years ago I trod the sand
In Summer, one of a gay young band,
Just to see, at lowest ebb of tide,
Two or three stones by the sea-marge wide,
Never dry, sand buried, seldom seen,
Last worn relics where the church had been.
How vain our days!—Time's too-skilful hand
In life's hour-glass has lowered the sand;
Turned laughing girls into women staid,
And my hostess still and low has laid!
Yet, Uncle mine, you tell me, long ago
You played, a child, where the wild waves flow;
In the churchyard, with its soft, cool breeze,
You chased the butterflies and wild bees,
Despoiled the beetles of their bright mail,
And gathered the wild flowers sweet and frail.

To Daniel Dunn,
*   Leeds.*

May 21.

DO I LOVE THEM *NOW* AS *THEN*?—

Do I love them *now* as *then*?—
Wildlings fair of wood and glen,
Flowers that flashed earth's beauty dim
From the rivulet's cool rim ;
Giving beauty's first sweet gain
In fair floral shade and stain,
Ere the sense of pain and doubt
Circled earthly joys about !
Then I loved them as a child,
In one joy all sense beguiled !
Now experience gives no joy
Without some shadow of alloy—
Faint heart-thrill of pensive pain
Wrapped up in rose-petal's stain !
Now in folded bud and leaf
Some life-sermon claims belief,
And the violet's sweet Spring-breath
Tinctured is with Autumn's death.
Much of legend, much of lore
Gathers in my floral store—
But life, knowledge, culture, art,
Do not childhood's love impart.

*To my Aunt Mary Dunn,
Easington.*

May 22.

A TOUR IN IRELAND, 1776-1779,
By Arthur Young.

Against our long-continued rule of wrong
This book brings condemnation clear and strong,
And lays a heavy load of sin and shame
Against those who were Irish but in name;
Whose base and selfish toil through long, dark years
Drew in red gold, and scattered grief and tears.
The landlord's sin, the law, lax or severe,
The people's genius, good or bad, doth here
Find calm, clear statement, worthy all belief,
With warning of the just entail of grief.
Young well performed a service, for no meed,
That might have proved regenerative seed
To bear rich fruit of honour to this land,
And sad Ibernia's faith and love command.
He left no problem to perplex the fool,
But gave the breach and mending of our rule;
Claimed for the monied wrong a stringent law,
And for the peasant safety from his foe!—
Rich rulers haste not to relieve from wrong
The poor, whose freedom shall proclaim them strong.

To W. R. Christie,
    Hull.

May 23.

THE PIRATES OF THE HUMBER.

We conquered them far out at sea !—
They made no vain attempt to flee ;
Met us like fiends, with sword and pike,
The sort of foe a man may like
Who bites the bloody hem of strife
From utter weariness of life.
A few we spared—but how, Mars knows,
Amid that storm of slashing blows !—
Pale, blood-stained, tottering, and half-dead,
Claimed by the law, their sentence said,
We led them forth one sunny day
The stern death-penalty to pay !
Gibbets were fixed along the marge
Of cliffs that breast the wild sea-charge,
And there we strung them, scarce a word
Uttering as we fixed the cord !
There, long years through, in stormy blast
They hung, until decayed at last,
The white bones lay upon the earth
Awaiting God's strange second birth.

To T. J. Monkman,
    Hull.

May 24.

HISTORICAL NOTES ON SHORTHAND.

In high respect he held shorthand,
Old Fosco of the massive mind,
But of the unheroic brand.

Among the princes of the land
He moved, good paying freights to find,
And keep a balance well in hand.

Of letters he had small command,
For Nature never had designed
His words to be his meaning's brand.

His flow of language was not grand,
And doubtless he was oft resigned
To classic Hades—in shorthand—

By those who toiled at his command,
And vainly strove his sense to find,
Whose words were not his mental brand!

Then on high ground he'd take his stand,
And vow he never had designed
The words that met him in longhand—
Old Fosco of the heavy brand.

"Historical Notes on Shorthand,"
  By J. W. Gould,
    Hull Literary Club. 880.

May 25.

THE SALLY ON BEVERLEY, 1642.

Oh! what hurry and scurry and riot
   When we marched into Beverley town,
How we laughed when we saw the gates open,
   And knew that the drawbridge was down—
For none seemed to heed or to hear us,
   Till the guards were attacked and o'erthrown.

Oh! what hurry and scurry and riot,
   When they rushed to repel our attack;
What shouting and clashing of weapons,
   Intermixed with the pistol's sharp crack,
As bravely we strove to press forward,
   And as bravely the foe bore us back.

Oh! what hurry and scurry and tumult,
   When foiled, and in desperate flight,
We re-entered the gates of our fortress,
   Friends greeting us back with delight.
But our hearts were sore stricken with sorrow
   For the heroes who fell in the fight.

                                  D. D. LAMPLOUGH.

To *Miss A. M. Blythe Robinson,*
    Lairgate,
       Beverley.

May 26.

RAVENSPURN.

Ravenspurn! Sea-port of the dead!
O'er thy memory ages spread
   Dust and ashes of spent time!
Thou art reft, forlorn, forsaken;
By the fierce, wild sea-storm shaken
   To a ruin half sublime!

Ravenspurn! thou stronghold riven,
Ramparts stern to ruin given;
   All thy glory brought to doom!
Dream we of that ancient glory,
Of thy mediæval story,
   Ere thy sudden death-night's gloom!

Ravenspurn! thou sea-port storm-beat
Into fragments by the sea-fret,
   Lost and hidden in the wave!
Honour, merchandise, and gold rest
Underneath the wild waves' cold crest,
   Swallowed by an unknown grave!
Stormed and ruined by the wild sea,
Rolling, age-long in its glee!

"*Ravenspurn,*"
  To Captain John Travis-Cook,
    Hull Literary Club.

May 27.

POPISH RECUSANTS BROUGHT TO HULL.

> WHAT is their crime ? What deed of blood
> Casts them adrift upon this flood
> Of wrath and hate ; so wan and pale
> That soft compassion should prevail
> O'er rage, and soothe their deep distress,
> Were their dark inner crime the less.
> They are Recusants—Ah, you start !
> That stone went crashing in the cart.
> Blood on his face—you like it not—
> Speak low, this is a crowded spot.
> They cannot bring their conscience down
> To own the God-head of the crown—
> Perchance dispute Eliza's claim
> To Henry's crown and Royal name.
> Honest ! you say. But then, my friend,
> Such honesty brings shameful end.
> They near the prison ; welcome rest
> To recompense their soul's protest.
> Be sorrow short—the dungeon's gloom
> Is but their gateway to the tomb.

To T. *Brocklehurst,*
    Hull.

May 28.

HULL WITCHES.

To be forsaken, old and weak,
Dark witchcraft's horror did bespeak
   In England's good old time.
Strange that the young, and rich, and fair,
Escaped the Tempter's dazzling snare,
   And never wrought the crime!
We know they seized the poor and old—
In the town's records it is told—
One, with pillory's filth besprent,
To a deep dungeon's gloom was sent.

Witches enough, with sparkling eye,
Soft cheek and lip of ruby dye,
   Wrought mischief in the town!
Indulged in frolic, song and dance,
Set strong men by the ears, perchance,
   But no one put them down!
'Twas bad, this heaping crime on age
Too weak to thwart the foul outrage,
Yet grace to two poor creatures shown
Speak great things for our good old town.

To Thos. Norman,
   Hull.

May 29.

AT WALTON HALL, 1864.

Yes, something more than two decades
Have passed their pleasures and death-shades
O'er our young lives since that green May
That lent us one gold-flooded day,
With Walton Hall and its domain—
Gay tinted with the young Spring-stain !
The gold-flush of the sky, the air
All perfumed, and the flowerets fair,
With birds and insects thronging round—
Life-treasure of that sacred ground—
Are mine again ! and I behold
The water-gate, war-battered, old,
That felt the storm of war and hate
Which bore the Stuart to his fate !—
Young beauty's flush has changed or sped,
Some sharers of our joys are dead ;
And Waterton takes death's long sleep
Where the two old oaks above him weep :
And I reap pleasure to this day
From the old memories of that May.

To J. A. Bray,
    Goole.

May 30.

THE RESTORATION.

Not by valour, not by might,
Triumph of the fierce death-fight,
   Came that happy day!
Not with victor's wreathèd bay,
Captured flags in proud display,
   'Neath the sunny May!
None could make the martial boast,
   " We the rebels hold
'Neath our heel, from coast to coast,
   Fettered, young and old ! "

Valour that so oft had sold
Its stern merit for red gold,
   Knew not that disgrace!
Pity we the people's shame,
And the selfish monarch blame,
   Blotting that high place
Where his father chose to die,
   The unconquered King!—
And great Cromwell, lifted high,
   Proved ambition's sting!

To Markham Spofforth,
   London.

May 31.

THE REV. JAMES SIBREE.

As Moses, 'twixt the living and the dead,
In years swept dimly down the tide of time
I see thee standing in thy manhood's prime,
Praying by open graves, with reverent head.
Above the town contagion's veil is spread ;
Death-terrors still the hopeful marriage chime,
And love, in tender offices sublime,
Tends watchfully the sufferer's dreadful bed.
From grave to dungeon ! Fighting cruel wrong,
With prayer and earnest action, to restore
To God's fair earth the victim of the strong,
I see thee labour, and, the conflict o'er,
Rejoice with Colborne, object of thy long,
Brave toil of mercy, that threw wide the captive's door !

To the Rev. James Sibree,
  Author of " Recollections of Hull."

JUNE.

Rose-flush upon a maiden's soft, warm cheek,
   Sweet bird-song in the happy paths of June,
   All earth responsive to the low, glad tune,
Too shyly timorous all its love to speak!
Sunshine, that woos the throbbing earth to seek
   Expression in the green year's gentle noon.
   Clothe her fair brow with light, her beauty's boon,
Who thrills to love, so innocently meek!
Dreams, soothe her spirit in your fair embrace,
Hope, deck the pathway of her sleeping years,
   Love leading her with firm, but gentle hand!
Ah, laughing June! her innocent sweet face
Dash with the dewdrops of thy fresh, warm tears—
   The sweetest bride in all the sunny land.

To Patty Honeywood,
        Leeds.

June 1.

"RAMBLES AND MUSINGS."

Fresh is the Spring with bud and bloom,
And odour chaste of young perfume—
The promise of the virgin year,
All bloom-flushed through its crystal tear—
So Waller waves the lilac fair,
And bids us banish wrinkled Care!

Fair is the Summer's golden hem,
And rich her floral diadem;
Her flowing robes are bathed in dew,
Her aureola's sapphire blue;
And at her feet the daisies white
Pour pearls and gold in their delight.

Fast follows Autumn, swarth and brown,
The bearer of a Roman crown,
In triumph guiding a huge wain
Where ripe fruits blush on golden grain;
Behind her stretch the stubble fields,
Before the storm its fury wields!
Here Waller shakes the poppies red,
And wreathes with vine his happy head.

To G. R. Waller,
  Wallsend-on-Tyne.

June 2.

AT THE THRESHOLD.

Little Elsie, sweet and pure,
Peeping shyly through the door,
At the path her feet must tread,
Ere God's "welcome home!" is said:
Bright green grass and sunshine clear
To her baby eyes appear,
With the daisy's pearly white,
With the swallow's circling flight.
Calm the sunrise of her day—
Scent of flowers around her way,
Song of lark and cool of breeze,
Fair green foliage of the trees,
Butterflies like fairies flitting,
Young birds on the branches sitting!
Soft green grass for baby-feet
Ere the mead and highway meet.
Little Elsie! life's dim quest
Soon must stir thee in thy nest,
But to-day our clinging arms
Closely press thy baby charms.

To Elsie Cook,
   Hull.

June 3.

SCARBOROUGH.

Old memories on the breezes sigh,
    And brood above the Summer wave,
The old years drifting slowly by.

Thy shattered ramparts pierce the sky,
    Our dim memorials of the brave ;
Old memories on the breezes sigh.

Serenely calm thy heroes lie,
    With dinted helm and shattered glaive,
The old years drifting slowly by.

O'er ruined walls the white gulls fly ;
    As ocean tempests wildly rave,
Old memories on the breezes sigh.

Life to thy ruins makes reply
    In tender vows by strand and cave,
The old years drifting slowly by.

Old days in crimson sunset die,
    New morning's gild the flashing wave,
While memories on the breezes sigh,
The old years drifting slowly by.

To Mrs. T. Tindall Wildridge,
    Beverley.

June 4.

YORK BLOCKADED, 1643.
(Sir Thomas Glenham's Protest.)

War presses fast to work our woe
  Whose banners late were floating far,
Field-wide defiant to our foe,
  Nor thought to droop behind this bar,
Where brave men throng too close,
Nor find fair field to use their martial force.

We sought not arms; yet were we glad
  For our King's cause good steel to draw;
Albeit our first pride grew sad,
  Friends, kinsmen, fronting us as foe!
Yet, swelling to the sky,
"For Honour, Church, and King!" arose our cry.

Sooner with Douglas would we hear
  Bird-song and twitter in the field,
Than squeaking of the mouse in fear,
  Close pent behind this fortress shield!
Give us the flashing front
Of war, when brave men dare the battle-brunt!

Not ours to choose! Our loyalty's high grace
All loss, save honour, shall for Charles embrace.

To George Knott,
    York.

June 5.

GREGORY THE OBSTINATE.

I HATE a crowd's unreasoning rage!—
You soldier, calm, sedate, and sage,
Pray what has yon old fellow done,
That thus his ears their curses stun:
Why stalks he proudly through the gate,
So calm amid this storm of hate.
Has he turned traitor, or a Jew,
That these poor fools make such ado?—
What! Sheriff made, yet would not stand,
Disdained the honour, your command!
Too bad! where is the fellow's taste?
No wonder that you bid him haste.
What! fined a hundred pounds, turned out,
Disfranchised—ruined, just about:
And by the Queen and Council's will,
The breezes here are rather chill;
Methinks I'll move—Friend, good-day;
Mind you are prudent, and obey!
My path lies through this open gate,
I'll leave these good folk and their hate.

To Councillor J. T. Smith,
  Hull.

June 6.

THE WALLS OF HULL.

Thy walls are fallen! With destructive hand
Time flung their strength in shards upon the strand:
Vain mediæval pomp, vain mural pride
Frowning defiance to war's surges wide.
One century's stain and fret retrace—here stood
Grim, mouldering ramparts, scarred by battle flood,
By Newcastle's fierce storm, when loud and far
Boomed the deep thunders of ensanguined war.
No glorious, warlike relics we retain—
Rampart, half-moon, or antique harbour-chain—
To prove the might, the terror of that time
When fierce revolt strode hand-in-hand with crime,
And the proud victor's crest was carried high
Against red banners and a scowling sky.
Then with barred gate, raised bridge, and guarded post,
The burghers dared, in arms, a monarch's host:
Edward and Henry's armies held at bay,
Nor dared their valour risk the dubious fray;
Once only victors triumphed o'er the town
When the stern Pilgrims tilted Henry's crown.

To W. H. Ingram,
  Manchester.

June 7.

OUTPOSTS AT HULL BRIDGE, 1642.

Here on this spot, one tranquil Sabbath night,
Charles urged the first waves of the fateful war,
Calm moon above, and many a silvern star
Shedding on helm and cuirass its cold light.
Soon the first ripples surged to tempest-height,
Breaking in flaming crests that spread afar
The ruin of grim wounds and death, to bar
Calm justice by the madness of red fight.
Slowly the great waves swept unto the sea,
Leaving a world of ruin on the beach,
War's red debris, sad wreckage of the strife,
With one great scaffold, the sharp sword's decree,
When the proud victor dared his King impeach,
And Charles surrendered sceptre, sword, and life.

To Col. B. B. Haworth-Booth,
   Hull Bank House,
     Hull.

June 8.

SIR ROBERT HILDYARD.

In Winestead Church, beside his lady wife,
   The good knight slumbers through the world's unrest,
   The sword, the shield, the helm's despoilèd crest,
Laid by, no more to stem the tide of strife.
Fair knight of fertile Holderness! his life
   Was edged by warfare's fierce and bloody quest,
   As York, with awful fury, wrought to wrest
The crown from Lancaster, with sword and knife.
The leader of a wild and fierce revolt,
   That dared the block, and held the sword at bay,
'Mid death-drift of the feathered-shaft and bolt,
   He heard the last loud trumpet close the fray,
As sunset shadows crept o'er mead and holt,
   And peaceful bells tolled out his life's long day.

To Councillor J. Brown,
    York.

June 9.

DEATH OF ARCHBISHOP SCROOPE.

Had we lost him in the lurid light
When the crimson sunset heralds night,
And in the grey the first pale star appears
Above the stormy clashing of the spears,
Then we had rendered him with hands bathed red
From breast-gash, and wide harvest of the dead—
Rendered him as life's last sobbing gasp
Gave death the palm, and tore him from our grasp.
Alas! no crimson smote the green that day
To give the earth war's guerdon of decay,
But falsehood, with soft word and Judas-smile,
Around our manhood wove its bitter wile,
And won our good Archbishop, held so dear,
Without the reddening of a single spear.
To-day he died, amid the fair home-scene
At Bishopthorpe, as nature smiled serene
Beneath the gentle heaven's fleece-drifted blue,
And leafage, stirred when soft June breezes blew:
Then the rough block received his patient head,
By the rude headsman's axe so basely shred.

To T. M. Fallow, M.A.,
    Coatham House,
        Coatham, Redcar.

June 10.

AFTER THE PILGRIMAGE OF GRACE.

    Stern sorrow darkens all the north,
    With relics strewn of manly worth;
    Yet not deep grief for those who fell
    In battle's sanguinary swell—
    The tyrant shunned the battle throe,
    By snare and falsehood won his foe.
    He, the crowned thief, who sternly tore
    For his foul use the church's store,
    Casting sad monk and patient nun
    To poverty, this crime hath done!
    Far fouling the mild Summer air
    As murder lays corruption bare.
    The North is charnel with the death
    That bears contagion in each breath.
    Bereavement finds nor grave nor bier
    For the sad tribute of its tear.
    When judgment terrors flame the skies
    May those dead in condemnation rise,
    And the sad tears, so largely shed,
    Be fire-flakes on his guilty head.

To Jos. Gregson,
    Hull.

June 11.

BELLE VUE TERRACE.

Fled are thy pleasures now, Belle Vue,
    At memory's call to live again,
'Neath sunshine glad, and sky of blue,
As when thy parterres roses grew,
    Laburnums swung their golden-rain,
And life was pleasant in Belle Vue.

Sweet was the dream when love was true,
    Beneath the Lilac's tender stain,
Beneath the sky's unclouded blue.
Romance was potent to renew
    The glamour of Hope's smiling reign
When roses in thy parterres grew.

Before the years thy pleasures flew,
    Before autumnal storm and pain,
As life grew long and sorrow true!—
Thy peaceful homes are lost, Belle Vue—
    Lost is their music's gentle strain
As old years vanish in the new.

---

* Suggested by Mr. Clements Good's sketch of Belle Vue Terrace in the *Hull and East Riding Portfolio*, for June, 1887.

June 12.

EARL LINCOLN'S DEATH.

Far better had he died by black Dick's side
Than vainly poured at Stoke the red war-tide—
And yet methinks this wretched loss and stain
Less shame than riding in the Tudor's train.
The old stock had good blood, though vain and fierce,
Not careful where the dagger's point might pierce;
And Richard, with his cold and awful crime,
Went just too-far for even this dark time:
True, be it said, unto his knightly shield,
At Bosworth held the bravest man afield—
Shame was it Stanley gave his arm no chance
When burst his last fierce charge with spear and lance,
The Tudor then, with Brandon fairly slain,
Had left the crown for Lincoln's nobler reign—
The De la Poles, great, generous, and brave,
Seem doomed to failure and untimely grave!
Ah, well! we must this mushroom Tudor hail,
For loyalty goes with the latest gale,
In those mean times of change and frequent strife,
When hold we on poor tenure wealth and life.

To James Yates,
  Public Librarian,
    Leeds.

June 13.

OUR LOST BABES.

Sweet little babes that we held so dear,
Are you lost in the great world's fret and wear?
Whose lives were brief as the young Spring day,
With flush of blossom on sun-kissed spray,
That touched our soul with colour and scent,
With hope and promise divinely blent!
So calm 'neath shadow of broad blue sky,

Surely its promise should never die!
The sudden blast of an icy wind,
Or rain and hail in the storm combined,
And fair white petals are beaten down
With twigs and leaves on the storm-swept ground.

Summer shall pass with its crown of gold,
None of your fruit shall its sway unfold!
Our babes, like blossoms, have sped away
In death-storms cold of the young Spring day,
And Summer will miss no tone of glee
In meadows fair where the babes are free—
But, dear lost babes! in our inmost heart
You are hid so deep we can never part.

To W. J. C. Nibbs,
    Portsmouth.

June 14.

A MEMORIAL.

Day-dreams and Summer joys depart
   As twilight shadows gloom our way,
But sweet song lingers in the heart.

As Time, the Parthian, hurls his dart,
   And grieves our twilight with decay,
Day-dreams and Summer joys depart.

Soft echoes from the distance start,
   Far coverts of life's golden May,
As sweet song lingers in the heart.

Low echoes of the Poet's art
   In life's dim twilight softly stray—
Day-dreams and Summer joys depart!

Far strays the hum of quay and mart,
   We wander by wild cliff and bay,
As sweet song lingers in the heart.

Ah! olden strains that did impart
   Glad music to life's golden May!
Day-dreams and Summer joys depart
But sweet song lingers in the heart!

To the late Aaron Smith,
    of Hull.

June 15.

THE DEATH OF SIR JOHN MELDRUM, 1642.

    Haul our fluttering banner half-mast down,
    Sad death-signal for the waiting town ;
    Oft repeated in these war-like days
    With their sieges, storms, and lesser frays !
    We have followed where he stoutly led,
    Glittering battle-surges breaking red ;
    Cannon wildly booming, flank and rear
    Threatened by the gallant Cavalier.
    Never falt'ring, true heart all aflame,
    With us honour's lasting sum to claim :
    Winning step by step with sword and spear,
    Through the serried column passing sheer,
    By the dint of weilded point and edge ;
    All atoss, like winter-beaten sedge,
    Pikes and banners of the scourgèd foe ;
    Drifting, eddying far the white-smoke flow.
    Died at Scarboro' torn by lead and steel
    In the wild rush of the battle-reel !
    Honoured by us of this good old town,
    Haul our tattered banner half-mast down !

To W. Smith, F.S.A.S.,
    Morley.

June 16.

ON THE DEATH OF CAPTAIN WILLIAM NEWTON, 1886.

After life's storm and travail past
The sailor enters port at last ;
Not bronzed and grey with weight of years
Nor weary of the sea-storm's fears ;
But resting on a tranquil shore
On wild sea-travel bent no more,—
Blest with prosperity's fair noon,
Why should death close his day so soon ?
While votive wreaths bestrew his bier,
And falls the tributary tear,
Old friends recall the distant day
When angry seas restored their prey,
And deep excitement seized the town
As the " Excelsior's " fate was known.
Suspense had passed to silent grief
Ere came our sorrow's strange relief—
The story of the six days' strife
Between encroaching death and life,
When rescued from the spray-swept mast
From death's grim jaws the sailor passed.

June 17.

A TRAGEDY AT BEVERLEY, A.D., 1385.

Here ages past grim passion smote a blow
That laid the hope of manhood in the dust,
When reverend age before the throne bent low,
Claiming the block's requital, stern but just:
Whereat the King, soul-stricken, bade the law
Its terrors hurl on guilty Holland's head,
All Knighthood silent, in a maze of awe,
While wide and far the dreadful news was spread;
One mother bore the murderer and the King;
In agony she claimed the royal grace,
Death smiting her fond heart with sorrow's sting,
Ere mercy moved her suffering to embrace:
Through heart-break thus the mother sought her tomb,
While Knighthood hailed dark Holland's haughty plume.

To James Mills,
    Town Clerk, Beverley.

June 18.

FLAMBOROUGH.

Rock-ramparted, and fenced by stormy seas,
In Winter, torn and smitten by the gale!
In Summer, with fair sea and passing sail,
Thou art the very realm of tranquil ease!
Here dreaming Fancy woos each gentle breeze
In sweet solicitude for love's soft tale,
But Truth's stern voice swells to the wild death-wail,
As roaring tempests the frail vessels seize.
The storms of centuries score each fretted cliff,
Grim caves the fury of the sea attest ;
Dark vestiges of wreck are on the strand,
And from the Head the grey tower, stern and stiff,
Speaks in its strength of strife and wild unrest,
Of battle-surges breaking on a ravaged land.

To W. H. Goss, F.G.S.,
   Stoke-on-Trent.

June 19.

THE HULL SUBSCRIPTION LIBRARY.

The genius of the living and the dead
Is stored within these walls, our priceless gain,
Won by the student's, the explorer's pain,
With heart-ache sore, and throbbing of grey head:
Won with what joy, sun sinking low and red
Behind the surges of the western main,
After long search through nature's maze and stain—
Perchance the martyrs sigh, the victor's bed,
A Cranmer's crown, a Wolfe's most glorious day,
Speak to the heart from this dim, yellow page;
While here a poet calls us to rejoice,
A thundering Knox exhorts us to obey,
And the sweet pleading of some ancient sage
Blends with the dignity of Darwin's voice.

To Alfred Milner,
    The Librarian.

June 20.

BEREAVED.

I do remember when, with mournful tears,
I laid my first sweet babe to solemn rest—
Sky-bird that could not brook an earthly nest—
You smote few words upon my weary ears,
But gave the sympathy that time endears—
The silent heart-touch that we love the best,
Until, eyes clear, we see the angel-guest,
And wait the slow, sure comfort of the years.
Now the Death-Angel's wings have passed above
Your babe's wan face, and from its restful sleep
It nevermore shall wake the heart of love
By baby-tears that make the strongest weep.
Our babes have passed our wisdom, to reprove,
Perchance, earth-clingings that we vainly keep.

To Chas. and J. Haselden,
      Hull.

June 21.

SUMMER.

'Tis glowing Summer! from the sunny clime
    She came, the follower after jocund Spring,
    Which made our vales and budding woodlands ring
With music. Though those stirring lays sublime
Are nearly ceased, (but to resume in their due time),
    Yet joyousness doth peaceful Summer bring
    To all, if nightingales no longer sing,
And thrush's voice is past its dulcet prime.
The eye is upward cast to a clear sky,
    So cloudless, quiet, and intensely blue.
Then as the Sun sinks ere the twilight hour,
    The western sky's a living flame; yet few
This passing scene receive—this heavenly dower,
God's gift bestowed, for every human eye.
                                    J. R. TUTIN.

To Miss M. J. Tutin,
    Fencote.

June 22.

THE PICTURE OF A SUMMER-LANE.

Won from what golden Summer's gentle prime
Is this fair, peaceful scene, this country lane,
So wealthy in lush grass and leafy stain,
And old gnarled trees, whose sprays of ivy climb,
Like patient pilgrims of a love sublime,
As though intent the azure heights to gain,
Where like a God the blinding sun doth reign—
Dispenser of the wealth of Summer-time!
Clay, dust, and ruts are hemmed with strong green grass,
And hedgerow-thorns, of lichened, knotty limb,
But green above, where Spring-time snows were shed,
And haws shall redden as the late days pass,
And Autumn glories fade, her skies grow dim,
As nature broods, and storms rage overhead.

To George Cammidge,
    Artist, Withernsea.

June 23.

BEVERLEY DURING THE PEASANTS' WAR.

John Ball and Tyler shall amend our wrong—
The tower and city theirs, a mighty throng,
Daily increasing, as the peasants drift
Londonward, the rude scythe-spear to lift
Against the Lords, devourers of the spoil
Delved by our labour from the grudging soil.
This brother came last night, sharp perils past,
And brought this burthen of good news at last.
Now let us form our ranks, no more delay ;
Great be the peril that shall bar our way !
The nobles, wont to flash the spear and shield,
Bar their strong gates, deserting the wide field.
There's been no battle—few the blood-drops shed—
Perchance a judge or lawyer's lost his head !—
What messenger is this, who follows fast
Upon his tracks who brought good news the last !
What ! Tyler slain, our brethren scattered, fled—
Heaven's curse be on the victor's guilty head !
Heaven, earth, no succour bring !—yet take your steel,
One brave stroke each shall work our misery's long repeal!

To Edwin F. Wiley,
  Brough.

June 24.

EARL MORTON'S VISIT.

Here rides Lord Morton—Listen to the cheers!
No, none of mine; I'd sooner lose my ears.
Guide him, good Sheriff, through strong Hessle-gate,
Under the gallows tree, hinting his fate.
Why should this Scot be thrust under our nose?
Who honour our Queen and keep our old laws.
Think of his faith!—With his neck to the block
At high Heaven's gate he'll make his first knock.
Haven't we rogues enough, true English born—
Hadn't we better put this to the horn?
Brave! did you say? Yea, our gallows-tree old
Oft dances such heroes out in the cold.
Are brave men so scarce? Why here in our town
Have we not heroes of equal renown?
Foul fall the day when men gallant and good
Find their just claim to high honour withstood.
Why should we honour the wicked and bold,
Vainly pretending mere copper is gold?
Crime and rebellion dishonour his name—
All our loud plaudits won't cover his shame.

To Fred. W. Holder,
      Hull.

June 25.

IN SANCTUARY AT BEVERLEY.

The cross is over me! repealed, I live—
It dawns how Jesu's mercy doth forgive!
At midnight, crouching in the house of God,
A wounded man, beneath sin's iron rod!
I hear the shrieking storm, the thunder's boom,
Late panting through its fury from my doom.
Stern men behind me pressing, swift and strong,
To claim my life's requital for their wrong.
I cannot see—all forms are bathed in night,
Save one red hand that will not leave my sight.
Alas! that one wild moment's rage should close
My soul in these fierce agonizing woes!
Bring shame upon my father's honoured name,
Blight every prospect of my spirit's aim!
A wife's, a mother's bitter tears are shed
For the poor wretch whose foolish years are fled!
His babes, poor innocents! with mine may weep
The hate whereby such bitter fruit we reap.
Ah, see! his eyes glare fiercely through the night,—
Oh, Mary! Mother! shield me from the sight.

To Joseph Dodgson,
  Leeds.

June 26.

THE BURNING OF BAYNARD CASTLE.

Have you heard that story olden?
  But a legend now, we say;
Yet within its myth enfolden
  Bearing honour's silvern ray.

Unto Hull the monarch high came,
  Louted round the supple herd!
Praised they Lord Wake's beauteous shy dame,
  Till the monarch's heart was stirred.

" Let Lord Wake at once be bidden
  For our visit to prepare!"
Quoth the King, " The prize thus hidden
  Touches us, who love the fair!"

Wake, who loved his lordly stronghold,
  Gave it promptly to the flame,
Prizing more than fame and red gold
  His high honour and fair dame!

Then the monarch, little guessing
  Whence the flame and ruin grew,
Sent to Lord Wake, red gold pressing,
  His fair castle to renew.

To Thos. Brayshaw,
  Stockhouse, Settle.

June 27.

THE REVOLT IN HOLDERNESS.

Peal the bells! rouse the wide land—
Who'll obey such harsh command?
We will render just the aid
That in justice may be made!
Have we ever failed the crown
When the Scot came swooping down?
Thought of ripe crops, wounds, or doom,
Marched in anger or in gloom?
Where's the use of donning mail
When no valour doth avail?
Let the King his foreign friends
Lead where battle-throe impends—
If they fall in their shed gore
We the battle will restore!
Cheated, cozened, not again
Will we risk our honour's stain!
Let the Barons come in arms,
Holderness rings with alarms!
Yeomen gather, bridges fall,
At Sutton Grange meet we all.

To Alderman S. Woodhouse,
  The last High Constable of Holderness.

June 28.

ANLAF ENTERS THE HUMBER.

With flowing sail and straining oar
Up the broad Humber Anlaf bore,
  Soul-mad to pull down Athelstan
And on his own broad, kingly brow
The honours of the crown bestow.
  From beacons red the warning ran!—
Bright armour gleamed by fen and crag
Beneath the wide-spread Saxon flag;
  And soon arrayed in battle guise,
With thick death-sleet of flint and dart
The drifting war-floods forward start,
  With thunder of wild battle-cries.
The lapping surges fret to foam,
Dark blood-flakes strew the beaten loam,
  Where Kingly Anlaf heads the van,
And, high above the level spears
His broad black Raven-flag appears!—
  Above the helm of Athelstan
The dying day's red beam is shed,
A victor he, 'mid hosts of dead!

To the Memory of Simeon Rayner,
    Pudsey, Nr. Leeds.

June 29.

A LEGEND OF THE PRESS-GANG.

Newland's maidens, joyous and fair,
Filled the breath of the summer air
With the merry music of laughter gay,
Tossing on high the scented hay;
When, loud and clear, a cry for aid
Caught the ear of each winsome maid,
Who, to her womanly instincts true,
Over the meadow quickly flew;
Modest or timid, neither stayed,
Rushing to render willing aid
To where a seaman lay forlorn,
By the cruel press-gang overborne;
Their pointed hay forks deftly plied,
Turning the ruffian gang aside;
And as they held the foe at bay
Stopped a carrier on the way,
Then trooping arms with martial pride
On through the busy town they hied,
Filling the streets with their merry cries,
Escorting home their grateful prize.

D. D. LAMPLOUGH.

To J. N. Dickinson,
Park Lane, Leeds.

June 30.

THROUGH THE WINDOW.

Through that olden window seen,
  What gay pageants caught the eye,
Scenes of triumphs that had been.
Seldom was the sky serene,
  Oft the dead leaves drifted by—
Through that olden window seen.
Then the dreamer caught the sheen
  Of bright lances in the sky—
Scenes of triumphs that had been.

Sweet song did the watcher glean
  From the twilight's stormy dye,
Through that olden window seen,

Where the falchions, flashing keen,
  Girt the banners floating high—
Scenes of triumphs that had been.

Sorrow came, with gloomy mien,
  Changed the song, and did deny
Dreams of triumph that had been
  Through that olden window seen.

To Miss Minnie Hyde,
  Hull.

JULY.

Reigns the sweet Flora in her robes of state,
All gorgeous she, the glad year's happy queen,
With coronal of gold, long robes of green—
Smiling and tender, with deep love elate!
All happy creatures on her smile await,
So gracious the calm honour of her mien:
Blooms flush and wither in the Summer sheen,
Ripe fruits her golden noontide celebrate.
Ah, glad young matron, most serene and calm,
Served with such gentle homage of fair pride,
Tribute of budding bough and Summer fruit,
Pursue thy path ! Contentment s gentle balm
Born of thy love ! Hope flitting by thy side ;
Pomona pressing thy sweet lips in bland salute.

To John Ryley Robinson,
      Dewsbury.

July 1.

THE DEFENCE OF BRADFORD, 1643.

Plumes waved and rapiers flashed, a steely ring
To gird the stout men of old Bradford town,
Hard toilers, not to be put lightly down,
To cheer, against their conscience, for the King!
What could such rash revolt but sorrow bring?—
War-storm and cannon's roar, the victor's frown,
Wounds, suffering, death; war's debris, widely strown,
The anguish of defeat's deep, rankling sting.
They wrote their manhood on the era's page,
Discharged their freedom's bond in lines of blood;
First turned the surges of the foeman's rage,
And breasted, ere succumbing to the flood.
Well done! brave actors on a bounded stage,
Ye lost no honour, who so valiantly withstood!

To James Dewhurst,
   Bradford.

July 2.

CROMWELL'S CHARGE AT MARSTON MOOR.

CROMWELL! thy Ironsides charged well that day,
The red van all a hell of fierce affray;
Prince Rupert's cannon hurling death and woe
High o'er the head of our most stubborn foe,
While we reeled forward, smitten in the face,
Scored in the rear, and held from death-embrace
By the broad ditch and hedge beyond, aflame
With musketry, that tore us, blurred our aim—
'Twas then that thy psalm-singers spurred afar
Beyond the ditch and wide hem of the war,
To charge, with slackened rein, the royal horse
That spurred to meet the storm in its mid-course!
With wild sword-play and pistol-crack they tore
Their stern advance, 'mid death and streaming gore;
Reformed their ranks, with undiminished ire,
And rent the batteries' cloud of smoke and fire:
Cut down the gunners, when, relieved, our van
With new heart, and ranks reformed, began
To storm the ditch and hedge, a deadly bar
That held at bay the passion of our war.

To Major A. L. Flodman,
         Hull.

July 3.

THE CONSTITUTIONALIST.

I HOLD for Commons, Church and Crown—
Beware who strives to pluck them down!
The church is rooted firm and fast,
Strengthened through many a stormy blast.
Fair virtue and religion's grace
Its base and pinnacles embrace—
The prop and honour of our land,
Heaven-consecrated, it must stand.
Despite detraction wrath and sneers,
Through storm and passion of the years,
Divinity doth hedge the crown,
And glory gilds its old renown.
Our Peers in loyalty enfold
The shimmer of its antique gold,
And dare, with high, undaunted front,
Disloyalty's impassioned brunt.
The Constitution breasts the storm,
Elastic still to true reform—
My life and honour shall embrace
The rooted grandeur of its base.

To Frederick Brent Grotrian, M.P.,
  Hull Literary Club.

July 4.

JOHN TUTBURY'S DEFENCE OF HULL.

BOLINGBROKE has landed! Clad in arms
From Ravenspurn he marches. Wild alarms
Spread over Holderness, whose yeomen stout
Throng the usurper's fluttering flags about.
Now is the town in danger! Man the walls;
Stretch the stout chain where our good river rolls
Its volume to the Humber's turgid wave.
Plant Arbalast and Mangonal; the brave
Call forth in haste, with banner, bow, and spear—
Who wins the town by arms, shall win it dear!
Draw up the ships within the guarding chain,
Man them with archers, whose keen arrowy rain
Shall hold us safe, should foes attempt this point.
He will not storm!—The times are out of joint,
And we are bound to hold this bulwarked town
In all tried loyalty unto the crown.
Now friends! let us unto the walls, and draw
The bridges, that between us and our foe
The moat may roll, with wall and tower beyond—
They shall be filled who are of fighting fond.

*To W. H. Brittain, J.P., F.R.H.S.,
Ex-Mayor of Sheffield.*

July 5.

ON WHITBY SANDS.

Love comes to dream upon the sand,
    Beside the wide and changeless sea
That sweeps our footsteps from the strand.

Strength bends above a small white hand
    In chivalrous humility,
As love dreams softly on the sand.

Time whispers his low, calm command,
    And love has paid its golden fee,
As gentle footsteps leave the strand.

Time waves his fair enchanted wand,
    Fresh blossoms paint the emerald lea,
And love is dreaming on the sand.

Oh, blushing face, by zephyrs fanned,
    Warm, faithful heart, no longer free!
Waves sweep our footsteps from the strand.

Yet true-love takes a higher stand,
    Beyond this cruel, changeless sea,
That breaks upon the Summer-sand,
    To sweep dear footsteps from the strand.

To George Clarke,
    Whitby.

July 6.

THE LANDING OF BOLINGBROKE.

Not to a wealthy town, with spire and quay,
Came exiled Bolingbroke, his quest a crown!
But by the sea-scourged causeway, widely strown
With wrack and fruitage of the sullen sea
That long had held Ravenser-Odd in fee,
His lordly banner to the gale was thrown;
Defiant he of fate or battle-frown—
The coronet or scaffold's harsh decree!
Ravenser-Odd was buried in decay,
Fretted to ruin by the ceaseless wave;
Poor augury for him on that far day
Who dared the might of Richard's arms to brave!
Oh sea! oh time! proved victors in this fray,
Ye pour oblivion o'er life's common grave.

Re "The Early History of Spurn Head,"
   By Lewis L. Kropf,
      Hull and East Riding Portfolio, June, 1887.

July 7.

RAVENSER-ODD: IN THE LAST DAYS.

Skies scowling in their stormy wrath above
Ravenser-Odd, enwrapped in surges white
Of black, far-swelling billows, whose fierce might
Stormed wall and pile, and swept the grave where love
And faith had seen the white wing of the dove!
While daylight touched the stormy edge of night
The priests, with host uplifted, awful sight!
Moved through the streets, with psalm and prayer to prove
God's help amid the rushing storm and sea!
Tossed, beaten in the drift of wind and rain,
The burghers toil behind in doubt and pain,
Still lifting through the storm their earnest plea
That God should lift his hand above the main,
And drive the billows back by his decree.

To S. A. Adamson, F.G.S.,
  Hon. Sec. Leeds Geological Association.

July 8.

TO THE MEMORY OF MY KINSMAN.
(Captain John V. Morris, slain July 8th, 1864.)

Three sons the old man gave, to hold
    The Federal cause, or die,
When fierce revolt in wrath unfurled
    Its banner to the sky.
And in the homestead there was grief
From bud to fading of the leaf—
The bitter strife was fierce and strong,
    Success was ebbing long,
Before the Union's iron might
    Wrought out in blood the right!

There was rejoicing unto God,
    Peace smiling through her tears,
When Freedom on the red soil trod—
    The triumph of sad years!
Then came two soldiers young and brave
From smiting wrath of battle wave!
But he, the first-born, grave and strong,
    From war had rested long!—
Slain in the clenching of the right,
    In the red van of fight.

July 9.

GLADSTONE.

Some statesmen claim their laurel for a day,
And live, forgotten, after its decay!
And some descend, heroic, to the tomb,
Green laurel mingling with their sable plume.
Frail men, whose sum of labour found its bound
Within their lifetime's short and changeful round.
Fresh swarms of such Ephemeræ rise each day
And claim the warmth and sunlight of their May.
Yet justly fame and honour we engage
For all who knew and served their own brief age.
They fill their niche beneath Valhalla's dome,
Their honoured page in the historic tome.
Greater than those there be, whose purer fame
Unto the earth becomes a sun and flame—
Whose radiant heat spreads far, a source of life,
Whose day-beam chases shades of closing strife,
Who, heralding a future, higher age,
Though full of years untimely leave the stage.
Such Gladstone's fame, whose herald star shall float
Far forward as earth's righteous law is wrought.

To Wm. T. Nettleship,
    Hull.

July 10.

SUMMER FRESCOES.

Cliffs, golden sands, a sunny sky,
White sails of proud ships speeding by.

Beyond the cliffs great wealth of grain,
Red mischief of the poppy's stain.

Green lanes a mass of leafy spray,
The scent of roses and new hay.

Green elm-leaves where the sunbeams flash,
The dark green glory of the ash.

The white moth in the twilight lane,
The gay Vanessa's varied stain.

The faint, rich scent of ripened fruit,
Young beauty of the maple-shoot.

The tranquil calm at evensong,
Night-dews where reeds grow thick and strong.

The glory of the harvest moon,
Far echoes of a low love tune.

To R. H. Philip,
     Hull.

July 11.

ROMANCE.

We lived it then!—grey castles on each steep,
Life's surges storming from a mighty deep;
A wild green earth, a changeful, stormy sky,
As night and day swept in fierce glory by.

We lived it then!—the glittering tournament
Presaged war's harvest, with rich blood besprent,
And when the fierceness of the storm was rent
Love smiled upon the poet's blandishment.

We lived it then!—the monk with artful pain
Inscribed it on white vellum for our gain,
And cut it in fine stone, on tomb and cross,
The strange dim story of Time's gain and loss.

We dream it now!—amid the smoke and roar,
The droning tumult of the city's core.
And to the devil our dreamland joys impart,
To gain the magic of the printer's art.

No matter!—life is sterling gold or dross,
We make the treasure of its gain or loss;
And win, perchance, in trying ages back
The fairest flowers that bloomed upon its track.

To Chas. H. Barnwell,
         Hull.

July 12.

VICTORIOUS.

Shut in !—Cold stone, and colder hearts,
Spirit from kindred spirit parts:
Low breezes and the gentle rain
For nature no sweet tribute gain.

Love, tremulous in soft caress,
The tombed and stricken cannot bless:
The midnight vision scarce may bring
A blessing on its transient wing.

Tombed—with the bitter curse of death,
And, still more bitter, drawing breath:
Heart, throbbing passion fierce and strong,
A pent volcano fed by wrong.

Curse turned from bitterness to balm,
The outraged spirit still and calm;
The nobler mind, sublimely great,
Reigning above the curse and hate.

From death a long bequest to life,
Grace beaten from the breast of strife;
A conqueror in a stony tomb,
A demi-god that shackles doom!

"*Prison Literature,*"
  By *A. Chamberlain, B.A.,*
    Hull Literary Club, 1888.

July 13.

COLON.

On dreamer! with the calm, grand brow,
Lined as the swift thoughts come and flow;
Deep eye that reads the tossing wave—
A new world waits the strong and brave.

Oh darkness of the deep, long night!
That breaks to no clear morrow's light—
Lo! fairer than an angel's plume,
A red light breaks the midnight gloom.

Sun of success! thy golden noon
Turns Winter into fruitful June:
Strong-heart the laurel on thy brow
Is fairer than the ruby's glow.

Oh Winter of our discontent!
How soon is Summer's fruitage spent!
Bear up, Strong-heart! thy iron chain,
Dishonouring less, shall honour gain.

Dim midnight of the tomb and grave!
Thou can'st not quell the great and brave:
The life returned—the name shall stand
The birth-right of a fair new land.

"*My Transatlantic Experiences,*"
By W. Barter, M.D.,
Hull Literary Club, 1888.

July 14.

TIME'S VICTORY.

Grimly mournful take thy stand,
   Triumphant o'er the dead,
Time, thou victor! whose strong hand
Ravages the smiling land
   Thy deceptive bounty fed!
Chasing Spring with Summer's gain,
Summer's fruit with Autumn's stain.

Art thou victor o'er the dead?
   Daring thus supreme to stand
By the tomb thy bounty fed,
When earth's rising sun was red,
   When earth's Spring-time nerved thy hand.
Hast thou won immortal gain,
Chased the laurel's vivid stain?

Time, thou reaper! 'mid earth's pain
   Thou hast won the weary dead,
Leaving earth her wisdom's gain,
Lore of sage and poet's strain
   That her offspring might be fed!
In our midst our great souls stand,
Clay alone falls to thy hand.

" Plato and Bacon, their Lives and Philosophies Compared,"
  By J. A. Patrick,
    Hull Literary Club, 1888.

July 15.

HISTORY.

A WILDERNESS of wood and men,
Wild war by deep flood and fen;
Wolf and boar with white death-fang,
Blasted trees where robbers hang.

Raised above the stormy field
Thorismond upon his shield—
Goth and Hun in slaughter blent,
Roman valour all but spent.

*Whirling Time from night to night
Thunders on in ceaseless flight.*

Round a city's wrack and shard,
Lo! a peasant ploughs the sward,
Baring skull and shattered sword
In the red earth thickly stored.

In his victor's pride elate
View the Kaiser's gory state,
Where red sabres hew and flash,
And the hot guns roar and crash.

*Still from ceaseless night to night
Thunders Time in hurried flight.*

"*History*,"
  By *C. C. Norman*,
    Hull Literary Club, 1888.

July 16.

THE LEGEND OF ROMELLI.

Bereft was she, in widowhood's sad night,
Her warrior husband sleeping still and lone,
To raise no more at trumpet's thrilling tone
The proud war-banner of his heart's delight:
One joy remained, one treasure blessed her sight—
Her brave boy in her heart, as on a throne,
Reigned graciously, and hushed her widowed moan,
Ruling and ruled by love's mysterious might.
So passed some little time, and then, alas!
Death, lurking in the Strid, waylaid his grace,
And cast a corpse into his mother's arms,
Whose gentle smiles to endless weeping pass,
O'er her dead child, held in her soul's embrace,
But gathered in by Christ from earth's alarms.

To Mrs. Garnett-Orme,
    Tarn House, Skipton.

July 17.

RICHMOND.

Sweep back dim change, sad ruin, and decay,
As Richmond's fortress in embattled pride
Frowns from its rocks o'er mead and river wide,
Floating its banner to the cheerful day.
Sweep on wild rumours of dark plot and fray—
Revolt, invasion, these strong walls deride!
We may the fury of the storm abide,
And with strong hand each haughty foe repay.
Alas! who fights with Time! whose silent force
Smiles in the changing seasons, calm and strong,
And wears alone his fair, unchanging crown!—
Grey ruins preach the rigour of his course,
Who silently retrieves our nature's wrong,
And calmly smites our loftiest temples down.

To the Rev. John Tinkler, M.A.,
  Arkengarthdale Vicarage,
    Richmond, Yorkshire.

July 18.

CIVIL WAR.

The glimmer of an evening star
Above the smoke and drift of war.

Sad twilight of a day of doom,
The flashing of a red war-plume.

A grey old grange in morning light,
A Cavalier for battle dight.

A fair girl frothing nut-brown ale,
The King's flag straining in the gale.

A sturdy Roundhead, pike at rest;
A flying steed, a shivered crest.

A battlefield, the silent dead;
A broken rapier, stained and red.

The reading of a dark death-roll;
A sable block, a headsman tall.

A monarch's bier, a useless crown;
A pale girl in a sable gown.

To the Memory of Walter Thornbury.

July 19.

THE LORDS OF HOLDERNESS.

"Lordings, there is in Yorkshire, as I gesse
A mersh contree ycalled Holdernesse,"
O'er which the mists of time drift dense and low,
But gloom and lighten to the changing glow
Of war and dim invasion, as the Dane
Floats his red banner o'er the stormy main;
Or, with the flashing pomp of knightly spears,
Some claimant of the British crown appears;
Or Baliol, low ambition's abject slave,
To resting Scotia carries the red glaive.
The Lords of Holderness before us throng
Through time's dull drift, that veils the proud and strong,
Nor pours oblivion o'er the cot alone,
But drifts its shadow o'er the monarch's throne.
Where the baronial helmet flashes high,
Emblazoned banners drifting on the sky,
See the great Albemarle, with mailéd breast,
Head the triumphant van, red spear in rest,
And charge the flying Scots on Cutton plain,
Piled with war's debris red, its heaps of slain!

"The Lords of the Seigniory of Holderness,"
By F. Ross, F.R.H.S.,
Hull Literary Club, 1880.

July 20.

DREAMS.

I.

" This is the penal centre !" sad and low
The angel's voice that spake these words of pain—
And lo! there spread a broad and gloomy plain
From whose far centre shook a lurid glow,
From which there ever passed a silent flow
Of spirits, from whose souls the olden stain
Passed with each step that heavenward did attain!
So they moved forward, solemnly and slow.
" Is there no gulf to pass, and has the fire
No cruel hold, that they make no sad moan
Who late in that deep lake were bathed?" said I.
"Therein they lost wild passion, fierce desire
For Mercy melts thereby each heart of stone
To love and peace, with scarce one tortured cry."

To Michael Needler,
    Hull.

July 21.

DREAMS.
II.

AMAZED, I paused within that twilight land,
The far, external zone of God's abode,
Through which, like drifting snows, fair pilgrims trode,
Sweet amaranth branches budding in each hand.
" These pass from penal realms, by God's command,"
The angel said, " Sin's long tormenting load
Is shed in tears upon their pilgrim road,
Who soon shall in the light of Mercy stand!"
" But who are those, whose robes no lustre shed?"
I asked, " Whose hands no sweet green branches bear?"
" The denizens of God's external zone.
Mere theologians, in the letter dead,
Who lonely are, within the Father's care,
The last to swell mid-heaven's triumphant tone!"

To George Mackrell,
        Hull.

July 22.

ON THE HUMBER BANK, 1866.

DREAM, Summer, in thy joy and pride,
    Beneath the sky-pavilion's blue;
Old Humber flowing deep and wide,
    Its fair banks dressed in thy green hue!

Oh, Summer! dream of life's young day,
    Its hopes, its visions of delight!
With fair earth-lore and heaven's high ray
    To gild its sorrows in their flight.

Why should'st thou wake from such a dream,
    Beneath the rent breast of the sky,
From whose storm-clouds the blue-shafts gleam,
    And spread death-terrors as they fly!

Why, Summer! glooms thy sunny sky,
    Why spreads thy cloud of dim despair?—
'Tis but the veil that dims the light,
    The fitful prelude to the prayer!

To Miss C. S. Bremner,
    Hull.

July 23.

THE ROYAL COMMISSION AT HULL,
(EVIDENCE AGAINST DUDLEY and EMPSON).

Now are these men down!—take your fling
Beneath the shadow of the King!
I know your wrong; your word has weight—
Close in, with death-grip grim and tight.
Soh! you won't! Regard their doom
As fixed—before them surely gloom
Block and axe—likelier hangman's cord—
Tower-hill's the honour of my lord!
Their worst is done, and you and I
May safely pass the wretches by.
'Tis well, this rigour of the King,
To urge the rascals to their swing.
No doubt he'll keep his own hands clean—
But that, hereafter, will be seen.
I do distrust him—his dead sire
Shared these men's crime, and paid their hire.
Young Harry takes the gold they stole,
And aims—our good-will to cajole?
He would be popular, no doubt,
And storm all hearts—our champion stout.

To T. Appleton,
  White House, Hessle.

July 24.

THE SERVICE OF THE SHIELD.

Brave shields are rent, bright harness rust,
War pennons mildewed to green dust;
In holy church the sculptured tomb
Still stands, a text of change and doom.
On high the rusty helm and sword
Speak the honour of their silent lord!
Fair silken surcoat, shield of arms,
No longer gild the field's alarms!—
Proud chivalry's insignia lie
To relics shred, beneath the sky.
Still unto us the herald's art
Its old-time honour doth impart.
In the emblazoned shield we trace
The origin of lofty race;
The memories of war-trophies won,
Of feudal service nobly done;
Love's passion wrought to worthy end,
The hero's toil for King and friend!—
Thus in the tincture of the shield
Far flashes Chivalry's fair field.

*To the Memory of Maslin Kelsey Lowther,
    Langtoft.*

July 25.

THE LEGEND OF FORGET-ME-NOT.

Forget-me-not of pale, clear hue,
 From the fair Danube's dancing wave
Smile back the heaven's serenest blue,

Like Love's meek eye, in pearly dew,
 That wept the strength it could not save,
Forget-me-not of pale, clear hue!

Pure tempter of the brave and true
 Above the lost knight's tranquil grave
Smile back the heaven's serenest blue.

Death-token that his weak hand threw,
 Love's tender, dear bequest to crave—
Forget-me-not of pale, clear hue.

Though tremour of love's fears pursue
 Long parting of the fair and brave,
Smile back the heaven's serenest blue.

From one sad day what memories grew,
 What grace the cruel Danube gave!—
Forget-me-not of pale clear hue
Smile back the heaven's serenest blue.

To Mrs. William Andrews,
 Rose Cottage, Hessle.

July 26.

SIR JOHN ELLAND'S CRIME.

THREE homes he had made desolate that night,
At Crossland tarrying to take wine and meat,
The blood of its dead lord beneath his feet;
The trembling widow, sad, and deathly white,
Serving with wine this most abhorrèd knight,
Who pressed the dead man's little son to eat,
When the fair babe, in childhood's open heat,
Cast the accursèd bread with his frail might
Into the murderer's face! Whereon he swore
That it were well to weed Beaumont's fair seed
From out the earth, as weeds from springing corn.
Time passed, and no man testimony bore
Against Sir John, whose fierce and bloody deed
Was long heart-sorrow to that wife forlorn.

To W. H. Potter,
  Hull.

July 27.

THE SLAUGHTER OF THE ELLANDS.

The Elland's crime, wrought with the bloody sword,
Found red requital at their vengeful hands
Who were but babes when storm of flashing brands
Sprinkled red blood o'er hearth and board,
Each sad wife bending o'er her slaughtered lord.
Elland was tracked, and caught without his bands,
And with his life, for lust of blood and lands,
A poor requital made—this knight abhorred !
Next his successor, with his infant son,
Fell by the arrows of the wrongéd three,
When Quarmby and fierce Lockwood met their end ;
But young Beaumont with red hand safety won,
To cleanse his stains at Rhodes, beyond the sea,
Dying the red-cross banner to defend.

To Edward Dunn,
    Flamborough.

July 28.

MEADOW-SWEET.

To-day we'll search for Meadow-Sweet,
　　Gay rovers in that lush green lane !
Hemmed in by fields of golden wheat,
To-day we'll search for Meadow-Sweet,
The daisies crush with dancing feet,
　　And cull Forget-me-Nots again !—
To-day we'll search for Meadow-Sweet,
　　Gay rovers in that lush green lane.

To Annie. (A.E.L.)

OUR KATE.

Our Kate is studious o'er her book,
　　In Fairy-land she wanders !
You read it in her earnest look—
Our Kate is studious o'er her book,
From Fairy-land she gleans her stook,
　　And scorns your great commanders :
Our Kate is studious o'er her book,
　　In Fairy-land she wanders.

To Kate. (E.K.L.)

July 29.

DYSTICUS MARGINALIS.

His name is Dysticus, and he's
    A very Triton among Minnows!
He fiercely roams in limpid seas,
His name is Dysticus, and he's
Not difficult in food to please,
    This ravager of inland billows!
His name is Dysticus, and he's
A very Triton among Minnows.

To his Captor, Fred. (F.C.L.)

AN ACORN-CUP.

An acorn-cup, a sunny day
    Beneath fair elms and old oak trees,
The glad refrain of a song at play—
" An acorn-cup, a sunny day ! '
An echo of child-music gay
    That floats and dies on an Autumn breeze,
An acorn-cup, a sunny day,
    Beneath fair elms and old oak trees.

To Aunt Ellinor.

July 30.

AMŒBA.

Only Amœba! the merest speck
Of sarcode—call it a cell, this fleck
Of life that I bring before your mind
To prove the wealth of dim life we find
Who bend our cerebrum's grey-cell force
O'er single cells or a giant's corse.
It is contractile; draws up and out
Its pseudopodium, walking about
After some tiny speck of proteid,
To tuck into its sarcode, and so feed!
It's all nerve or no nerve, as you will;
Owns no cell-wall, but at heat's sharp thrill
Is irritable. It has no heart
But owns an outer and inner part—
Ectosark and endosark, to wit!
By fission—a scientific split
Right through its nucleus—it becomes two—
Perchance may multiply under view.
The contractile vesicle pray mark!
Also, it breathes—this queer little spark.
This is Amœba, whose form you view,
In structure and function resembling you.

To Dr. Dallinger, F.R.S., F.R.M.S, &c.,
  Sheffield.

July 31.

SCIENCE GOSSIP.

Old memories of wild fen and shore,
    Where valued friends in council met,
In genial gossip we restore.

Old faces beam on us once more,
    O'er microscopes in order set,
Their memories of wild fen and shore.

We view diatom, scale, and spore,
    And many a triumph and regret
In genial gossip we restore.

Our sage collectors tell their lore,
    Incur, discharge, the mounter's debt,
'Mid memories of wild fen and shore.

The " forms " Peru's guano bore,
    Fluid and balsam's gain or fret,
In genial gossip we restore.

We laud some gain, some loss deplore,
    Surmise what treasure we may get,
As memories of wild fen and shore
In genial gossip we restore.

To Dr. J. E. Taylor, F.L.S., &c.,
Editor of " Science Gossip."

AUGUST.

Ah, happy seed time! earth shall now return
In golden sheaves swart labour's cheerful pain;
The broad fields laden with their wealth of grain,
Where crimson poppies droop and burn.
Who would not 'mid such teeming wealth sojourn?
Glad, errant pilgrim of each leafy lane,
Lost in the worship of each deepening stain,
Gleaning sun-treasures for memorial urn.
Ah, sweet Maternity! wreathed in soft smiles,
With happy childhood clinging to thy hand,
Profuse in love, and wealth of ripened grace,
What tender joy the shortening day beguiles;
The tranquil calm that broods above the land,
Mirrored in thy serenely gracious face.

To the Rev. E. G. Charlesworth,
  Acklam Vicarage,
    Middlesborough.

August 1.

THE CAVALIERS AT HESSLE.

Toil on with spade and pick, 'tis for the King,
And when the fort commands the Humber's flow
We'll seize the nobler steel, and strike a blow
Shall make the Roundhead's stoutest harness ring.
With rapier's point, that seconds edge, we'll sting
Through double buff, until our gauntlets glow
With crimson stains, and prone in death below
Our charger's hoofs the stricken foe we'll fling.
Hark to the battle-drift from leaguered Hull,
Sweet music that makes light our heavy toil;
Meet presage of the laurels we shall cull,
Storming the battered wall, to slay and spoil
The Roundhead knaves, whose impious pride would pull
The crown to dust, and bathe in blood the soil.

To Jas. Baynes, P.H.D., F.C.S., F.R.M.S., &c., &c.,
Hull.

August 2.

YORKSHIRE NATURALISTS AT RICCALL, 1875.

Time floats between that day and this,
With glamour of its grief and bliss;
But through life's mirage comes again
The gold-flood of fair Summer's reign.
Far from the old world's roar and fret,
War-dight with vasculum and net,
By Ouse's flood, on Riccall plain,
We urge our gentle strife again :
From Flora win our trophies gay,
And make the insect-world our prey ;
Rehearse Hardrada's bloody fall,
When Riccall rang to wild war-call
And with broad forehead crimson-wet
Lay Tosti, his last frown death-set.
From war to peace—with kindly grace
And welcome of his genial face,
The vicar met, and led us o'er
The ancient church, rich in its store
Of relics—treasures of a past
Whose passion o'er our lives is cast.

To Thos. Birks, Jr.,
 Old Goole.

August 3.

MY FIRST VOLUCELLA PELLUCENS.

Volucella Pellucens this, a fly
Large, beautiful, but not of gorgeous dye,
Flashing metallic lustre in the sun
Until the summer of its life was done.
Embalmed in Balsam, on a crystal slide,
'Twill outlast me, and many more beside.
Observe that smoky-stain and broad, clear wing,
The abdomen's pellucid upper ring;
The slender ligula, deep-cleft and long,
Antennæ, feathered setæ, foot-pads strong,
And all perfections that the lens reveals—
Then ask his murderer what deep qualms he feels!
As counts the African each trophied skull
I hold my fly in balsam beautiful—
I see again its broad, barred wings outspread
'Mid florets of an umbelliferous head;
With far-extended arm and careful eye,
I make the skilful sweep and net my fly—
Again the music of its buzz I hear
Through lapses dim of many a year.

To W. G. Tacey, L.R.C.P., F.R.M.S.,
    Bradford.

August 4.

"QUEEN OF THE AIR."

Great poet of the subtle thought, no rhyme
Is needed for thy art, whose liquid time
Embraces all thy thought, as the rich sun
Embraces all things that beneath it run;

And unto all adds beauty, colour, grace,
Driving primeval darkness from their face,
Until the earth springs glad and new again,
Fair, virginal, and fresh in art and stain.

We lose the clouds, the shrines of Mammon fall,
The ages through the soft, sweet dawning call,
Greeting each other as in glad new birth
Life rises to the glory of the earth;

And knowing earth, to heaven draws gladly nigh,
Great in the spirit, since its purer eye
Beholds the Father's face, and sees His hand
Writing His glory in the gracious land.

As ne'er before through these Greek myths we see
The glory of the earth's theology—
Those worshippers who seeing not God's face,
Yet saw and held His hand in their embrace.

To J. W. Whiteley,
  Leeds.

August 5.

THE SEEN AND THE UNSEEN.

There is fruit that is hidden and fruit that is seen,
When Summer is changing her mantle of green;
But we glance on the days of the hopeful past Spring
For the promise that came with the birds on the wing.

The promise is sped, and the Summer is o'er;
How small is the sum of our fruitage in store!
The glory of Autumn is stormy and red,
Her harvest is gathered, her herbage is dead.

The wild wind is sighing, the earth is at rest;
The bird has departed—forlorn is her nest!
We count o'er the harvest in sorrow and pain,
Where much we expected how small is our gain!

We think of the wild wealth of beauty and bloom
When Spring, with a flood of warm light and perfume,
The green earth invested with beauty and praise,
And lightened with promise her fairest of days.

We knew not, poor toilers! the wealth of deep peace
That made up the sum of the harvest increase—
The beauty, the song, and the flow of perfume,
The spirit's true wealth that shall never consume.

To W. Pearson,
    Coltman Street, Hull.

August 6.

HORTUS SICCUS.

You thought them dead ! You little know
    The years that live in these dry leaves,
The memories that like perfumes flow !
You thought them dead ! You little know
Their wealth of Summer scent and glow,
    Their treasure of Autumnal sheaves !
You thought them dead ! You little know
    The years that live in these dry leaves !

Friendship and love around them cling,
    And memories fraught with rich perfumes !
Above them flit *Vanessa's* wing,
Friendship and love around them cling ;
Fulfilment of departed Spring,
    Each fadeless, treasured leaf illumes !—
Friendship and love around them cling,
    And memories fraught with rich perfumes.

To *J. F. Robinson,*
    Hull Literary Club.

August 7.

ROSES RED.

Roses red are Summer's fee!
  Beauty, flush thy snowy breast
With their spotless purity!
" Roses red are Summer's fee,"
Sweet birds carol from each tree;
  Fledglings twitter in their nest,
" Roses red are Summer's fee,
  Beauty, flush thy snowy breast."

Crimson hips upon the spray
  Tremble to the icy breeze!
Ruddy sunset gilds the day,
Crimson hips upon the spray
Prophesy another May,
  Bloom and scent of laden trees!—
Crimson hips upon the spray
  Tremble to the icy breeze!

To Mrs. H. Pattinson,
  Hessle.

August 8.

PROVE ALL THINGS.

Fair forms of beauty through the Spring-tide move;
Flowers bud, rich blossoms perfume rare impart,
Hopeful and glad the beating of my heart:
Life flutters on; why should I pause to prove
The joy that dances in a maze of love?
With the twin sisters, Nature and pure Art,
Far will I wander, and not one foul dart
Of sin shall gloom the sunshine from above—
Oh Summer, best beloved! thy happy reign
Is lost in storm and drifting of sere leaves;
Swart Autumn is bereft of beauty's stain,
No glad birds twitter in the cottage eves,
As, sighing, with unutterable pain,
Amid the ruin of lost years my spirit grieves!

"*Prove all Things. I. Thess. v. 22,*"
    By the Rev. John Holmes,
        Thornton Street Wesleyan Chapel, 1887.

August 9.

MAN.

Wrapped in the cloud-pavilion's sweep of blue,
Behold the round earth, mountain and river,
Lit by the gold-shafts from Apollo's quiver—
Soft light that doth the whole fair scene imbue.
The great moon rolls its shield of silvern hue
Where in the night-winds chill the woodlands shiver,
And the wild sea rolls its unrest forever—
All nature's charms in its soft light are new.
God, the Creator, utters His high law,
Obedient Nature works His sovran will!
See on earth's centre, child of doubt and awe,
Frail man, his narrow round of life fulfil :
Age-long the stream of life ebbs too and fro,
As the great system yields its wealth to human skill.

"*Man,*"
  By Councillor Fryer,
    Hull Literary Club, 1880.

August 10.

THE CHILD-WORLD—A BIRD'S-EYE VIEW.

You are in my heart to-day,
With your frolic and your play;
Flicker of your tresses gold,
Eyes so subtle, shy, and bold;
Sculpture of the dimpled limb,
Fair babes, at the grassy rim
Of the broad-life path that lies
Narrowing, lost in distant skies.
Fairy-palace, woodland, spire,
Sweet song-note of forest choir,
Soul-note of the poet's voice,
Call upon you to rejoice—
One long roll on daisied grass,
Then a sweet child-kiss, and pass
To the path that lies so fair,
Showing not one false death-snare!
Not one sorrow of the years,
Not one bitterness of tears;
All so calm in distant grace,
Not one evil can you trace.

To my Nephews and Nieces.

August 11.

RALPH WALDO EMERSON.

Subtle the sunshine that our joy reveals,
And on the passion of our spirit steals,
That flaunts before us bud, and leaf, and bloom,
And rolls the green earth in a glad perfume.

To daze our sense in luxury and bliss,
To touch and stir us with a honeyed kiss,
To start the spirit to new life again,
And crown it 'mid the sweet world's floral stain.

There is a wealth of sunshine that conceals,
A power that veils the magic that it deals;
The tissues grow, the budlings spread to bloom,
And myriad tiny cells shed their perfume.

A world of strength our nerves and muscles find
In the embracing of the unseen wind,
And the responsive spirit thrills to life,
In the baptism of an unseen strife.

So 'neath thy mind we grow! unconscious force
Strengthens our spirit for its unknown course;
We thrill to truths our inner souls retain,
While barely conscious how thy strength we gain.

To the Memory of James Pellitt,
    Master Mariner of Hull,
        (A Student of Emerson.)

August 12.

TRUE AND STRONG.

In the dim old days when wild war-flood
Rolled the wide Northland in ash and blood,
And the unknown dead, who sleep so well,
Relaxed not the death-grip as they fell!

Then the Northern heart was true and strong,
Ready to wrestle with arméd wrong;
To meet the storm of the Norman's rage,
Or bathe in his blood the battle-gage.

When lustful Harry, with crafty hand,
Despoiled the Church of its gold and land,
'Twas the fierce Northland burst into flame.
Though the liar foiled where he could not tame:

Dust of the centuries! cover the blood
Where roses crested the battle-flood!
While the glorious meed of Marston's day
Lives, though the centuries fleet away!

Yet the Northern heart is true and strong
As in the ages of storm and wrong;
And still the grip of the Northern hand
Is true as the steel of King Arthur's brand.

"*Phases of Yorkshire Character,*"
  By the Rev. T. Mitchell,
    Hull Literary Club, 1887.

August 13.

COLONEL ROBERT OVERTON.

Yes, some two hundred years have sped
Since in the gloomy Tower his head
Found for its rest a tranquil place,
And the Death-angel's solemn grace
Touched with its strange and subtle awe
Features paled by no meaner foe.
He stood against the King in war
That brought the monarch to the bar;
And flashed his sword in that dark hour
Which saw arrayed Newcastle's power
Around the frowning walls of Hull,
That through the fierce storm, beating full
On tower and rampart, spake in flame
And thunder for its ancient fame.
He gave the passion of his youth
For what to him was holy truth;
Opposed his sire—a King's man true—
And kept his faith the long war through,
Until disaster, failure, came,
And the death-dungeon—but no shame.

To Ald. J. W. Foster,
   Beverley.

August 14.

PRIMROSE DELL.

We know the haunt where fairies dwell,
    The sweet green nest of laughing Spring,
Where pale primroses star the dell!
We know the haunt where fairies dwell,
Where breezes rock the blue hare-bell,
    And Io spreads his jewelled wing!
We know the haunt where fairies dwell,
    The sweet green nest of laughing Spring!

To Bell, (J.A.L.)

FAIRYLAND.

Giants and fairies throng the brooks,
    The whole green earth is Fairyland!
You find them in dim woodland nooks,
Giants and fairies throng the brooks,
They hide within the harvest-stooks,
    And where the spotted foxgloves stand!
Giants and fairies throng the brooks,
    The whole green earth is Fairyland.

To Willie, (W.L.D.)

August 15.

MAY POSIES.

Now little West Indian, hold your hands,
   While I pelt you from the fields of May,
With golden buttercups, daisy bands!
Little West Indian hold up your hands
For lilacs pale and laburnum strands,
   Blue-bells cold and trifolium gay!
Now little West Indian, hold your hands,
   While I pelt you from the fields of May!

To Marion, (M.A.S.)

BESIDE THE SEA.

Oh, maiden in the Summer noon,
   Beside the golden sand,
What whispers float on the winds of June?
Oh, maiden in the Summer noon,
What is the slumberous sea's low tune,
   What is your heart's demand?
Waiting in your young life's noon
   Beside the golden sand!

To Miss Eunice Holland,
        Liverpool.

August 16.

MEMORIES.
(May 24th, May 14th, August 26th, and August 16th.)

They are not lost! those treasures of past years,
Though time has cast its shadow o'er the scene;
For as the cherished soul-love re-appears
The brown, sun-smitten ferns wave strong and green.
Where grassy mounds of death we dewed with tears,
Sweet violet and daisy white are seen.
And in the dim haunt of our Winter fears
Wild blossoms bathe and flush in sunny sheen.
The soul's sweet joy, its loving hope, returns
As in the old familiar paths we stray;
And love's sweet incense on the altar burns
To chase the charnel odour of decay,
As all along the sacred, solemn way
Sweet buds and garlands wreathe the funeral urns.

To the Rev. R. D. C. Cordeaux,
  The Vicarage, Paull.

August 17.

WILBERFORCE.

Sometimes we turn from those heroic days
When Nelson urged deep thunders o'er the wave,
Or when above the Belgian plain our glaive
Flashed like a meteor in the sunset rays—
Yea, turn, a dim doubt stilling our deep praise,
If we, who spurn the shackles of the slave,
May not have shed the life-blood of our brave
In wrath too prodigal, and stained our bays!
Dark is the doubt of blood and cruel war
That comes in orphan's tear and widow's moan,
But, Wilberforce! thy peaceful laurels claim
A wider homage, and no judgment bar
Shall turn to sorrow our laudation's tone,
The earnest tribute to thy righteous fame.

To the Rev. W. Spiers, M.A., F.G.S., F.R.M.S.,
London.

August 18.

NIGHT.

The gloomy night o'ershadows all the land,
Winds whirl above the surface of the lake
Until the very walls and pillars shake ;
Yet shall our crannoge many a storm withstand :
Submerged our causeway, our canoes at hand,
Our safety's long, calm slumber we may take
Until the tranquil morrow doth awake,
And toil or chase invite us to the strand.
Hard our condition, chipping with keen flake
Weapons that shall the forest-herd command,
Ring down the woodland's strength, and point the stake,
Or quell the onslaught of the foeman's band :
At eventide, with spoil from mere and brake,
In crannoge rest we, safe from beast and brand.

" The Lake-Dwelling at Ulrome,"
By Dr. T. M. Evans,
President of the Hull Literary and Philosophical Society,
Re the Hull Quarterly and East Riding Portfolio, April, 1885.

August 19.

THE RESCUE AT THE OAKS COLLIERY.

Who shall achieve the rescuer's noble fame,
And save a brother from death's sudden woe?—
Two youths stand forth—into death's realm they go—
Sparks rise, with frequent flash of ruddy flame,
And stern men knit their brows in wordless blame,
Scarce breathing in the deepness of their awe,
Nor doubting that the miner's deadly foe
Has won fresh triumphs, marring Mercy's aim.
All lost! And by the engine calmly stands
The father of one gallant boy, and waits
The issue—hopeful that the gloomy mine
Shall yet restore his dear one to his hands!
Faith wins!—relinquished of the deadly fates
The three rise from the grave to earth's sunshine.

To *Thos. W. Embleton,*
  The Cedars,
    Methley, Leeds.

August 20.

OLD PATHS RE-TROD.

So you, who heard deep thunders roar,
And stood amid the crash of war;
Who wandered ancient cities o'er,
Who heard the battle-thunders roar!
Returning to your native shore,
After sea-travel, wide and far—
You, who have heard the thunders roar,
And stood amid the clash of war—
Turned to the old school-days, and trod
With eager foot the olden way,
(Where still blue speedwells gem the sod
That in our old school-days we trod),
With slower step to homeward plod
From time's mutation and decay,
And sadly vow your foot had trod,
For the last time, the olden way.

To Edwin Bell, R.N.,
   H.M.S. Elk.

August 21.

OLD HEARTHS.

Old hearths grow cold, and the ashes lie
    Where the Yule lights leapt to ruddy glow,
For the dirge-like winds are sweeping by
    And the Autumn sun is sinking low.

The day-song ends in a weary sigh,
    Waters of bitterness ebb and flow,
For old hearths grow cold and ashes lie
    Where the Yule lights leapt to ruddy glow.

But bright stars rise in the cold night sky,
    Though hours of vigil are sad and slow;
The winds of the fresh young day shall blow,
The cold, dark night in the sunrise die,
Though old hearths grow cold, and ashes lie
    Where the Yule lights leapt to ruddy glow.

To the Rev. Edward H. and Mrs. Scott,
  St. Vincents, West Indies.

August 22.

ON CUTTON MOOR, A.D. 1138.

As the morn's grey mist grew thin
Closed our dark war-columns in —
A deep ring of bristling steel,
Strong to guard, or fierce to deal
Tender mercy of the fray,
When began the bright sword-play!
With a roar of battle-hate
Stormed the wild Scot to his fate,
Like an eddy's foamy swirl—
Rock-fast stood we in the whirl;
Spear at throat and guarded face,
Overhead the sword and mace;
Blood and wounds and ghastly death,
Dying men agasp for breath;
The heaving edge of our stern war
Wedged and dinted wide and far—
With the dead piled at our heel,
Circling high the impending steel—
Bore we up until defeat
Ended in their wild retreat!

To *J. B. Robinson,*
  Marsden,
    Huddersfield.

August 23.

A TRAGEDY.

A GOTHIC chapel, fair and sad,
In myths of saintly ages clad,
Where reverent age may slowly brood
O'er Time's sere leaves in solitude.

A brown monk, austere, wan, and lean,
A lady stately as a queen,
But bending in her tender grace,
To meet the lean monk's sad embrace.

A witness of his own deep shame,
With bound heart bursting into flame:
His iron will holds in command
The keen, long dagger in his hand.

Lo! red lips parting their embrace,
Upon them stares a death-cold face:
A few brief words of bitter hate
Bear burthen of a double fate.

A brown monk quivers on the floor
That takes the stain of spreading gore;
The stern grip of an iron hand
The lady's faltering steps command.

To H. Pattinson,
    Hessle.

August 24.

THURSTAN'S CROSS.

It was a fearful day when Thurstan's Cross,
With sacred banners draped around its car,
Gleamed in the sunlight like a morning star.
Below, claymore, dirk, sword, and spears they toss;
Of human life tremendous is the loss!
Fierce rolled the surges of the Scottish War,
Shipwreck and devastation spreading far.
Swords clashed upon the shield, and target's boss;
All that long day grim massacre was rife;
But still the Cross stood high above the spears,
While all the field was dressed in glittering arms.
Fierce and embittered was the varying strife,
Till hard-won triumphs chased all doubts, all fears;
And the still night closed on the day's alarms.

To the Rev. Charles Best Norcliffe, M.A.,
    Langton Hall,
        Malton, Yorks.

August 25.

THURSTAN'S ARMY AT MALTON.

From Cutton moor's long turmoil of red fight
To Malton surged the fierce impetuous tide—
The Norman Barons in their steel-clad pride,
Pikemen and archers in their naked might—
A sad, but yet a memorable sight,
Where stains of recent battle did abide,
And valour failed the power of grief to hide,
Still faithful to maintain its manhood's right.
Fitz-John's stern vassals and the ruggéd Scot,
From wall and turret rang defiance far,
Armed to the death, intent with missile shower
To foil the storm, and urge, with courage hot,
The fierce defence, the sortie's stormy war,
And bar the might of Thurstan's righteous power.

To the Rev. Robert W. Elliot,
         Malton.

August 26.

A LEGEND OF OLD HULL.

Strong, fervent lovers of the chase were they—
Those Norman Kings, who held such haughty sway,
Hence the old legend that our town had birth
Through Longshanks running a poor hare to earth.
'Tis but a legend, lost in mist and rime,
A strange distortion of old father Time,
Disproved by learnéd Frost, who spared no pain
A clearer light for our behoof to gain.
Some truth the hoary legend may enfold—
Here pealed the huntsman's horn in days of old,
And Edward, running his weak quarry down,
May first have stumbled on the rising town.
Howe'er that be, the stag, the savage boar,
Oft o'er the plain or through the forest tore,
A haughty band in hot pursuit, with hound
And horn, that made the forest wide resound ;
When feathered arrow smote the swifter prey,
Or the rude boar turned savagely at bay,
And the fierce hounds, the hunter's ready spears,
Bore down the brute to storm of ringing cheers.

To W. Dearman,
  Hull.

August 27.

RAISING THE STANDARD.

No more vain talk—the keen edge of the sword
Is flashing bare, to prove who shall be lord!
At Nottingham our liege, the King, has cast
His proud, pretentious banner on the blast.
The augury was bad—day gloomed to close,
Few stood by him of all who aid his cause.
With little pomp, and few armed men in train,
The staff was fixed, and spread the broad red stain
Of the brave flag upon the heavy air,
When with dull moaning, as of death's despair,
The sluggish breeze rose to a swirling blast
That caught the standard's folds, and downward cast
Its proud emblazonry—its crown brought low!—
There was a long, deep pause of silent awe;
Then Charles, unaltered in the front of fate,
Bade them upraise the banner to its state.
Few were the cheers, and lacked the awful ring
Presaging triumph, as before the King
The flag streamed forth—a streak of bloody dye
Against the cold, death-dimness of the sky.

To Edward Dawson,
  Hull.

August 28.

THE STORMING OF MALTON.

Rang the loud trumpets, and the arrows flew,
Sweeping the ramparts of old Malton town,
In the dark days when Stephen wore the crown,
And o'er the north the winds of battle blew :
Then did the strong and fierce invader rue
Red, ravaged fields, with ruin widely strown,
As gloomed above them, with foreboding frown,
War's stormy clouds, eclipsing heaven's fair hue.
The missile hail, red flame, and driving smoke,
Smote fiercely and enwrapped their guilty war ;
Vengeance, delayed, but deadly in its might,
Crushing resistance with herculean stroke,
The shriek and roar of conflict flowing far,
Until day ebbed into the awe of night.

To William Constable,
  Malton, Yorks.

August 29.

OVERPLUS OF BLOSSOM.

Oh, happy Spring! thy coronal of bloom
Brings fairest promise to the waiting year,
That smiles in beauty through its crystal tear,
Emergent from old Winter's realm of gloom.
Too soon thy fleeting beauty and perfume
Are lost in storm-gusts where the leaves, dead, sere,
Drift to the wailing winds o'er Autumn's bier,
As Winter consummates thy certain doom.
We count thy fruit, a frequent, golden store,
Yet not thy blossoms full and perfect yield;
Our grey old roomy garners would hold more
From the gnarled orchard and the fruitful field.
Yet ample for all needs God's nature bore,
Nor aught of Spring-tide's promise to our loss repealed.

"*Overplus of Blossom,*"
  By the Rev. Robert Collyer,
    Park Street Unitarian Church, 1886.

August 30.

AN AUTUMN THOUGHT.

Here, where I drew my life's first painful breath,
Some restful years I fain would win, ere death
His noiseless hand sweeps o'er my little space,
And of my life and labour leaves no trace.

Here in the Autumn-tide, 'mid falling leaves
And stubble fields bereft of golden sheaves,
Sweet would it be to dream o'er old Spring days,
And view past pleasures through time's softening haze.

To roam secure by cliff and fretting wave,
To hear at eve the tempest fiercely rave,
And feel old passions past, old trials sped,
Then rest in tranquil peace my weary head.

Beside the green mounds in God's acre spread
To moralize without one thought of dread,
To see old faces thronging round me there,
Calm, purified from earthly stain and care.

To view life's mirage with one only sigh—
Grief o'er that sin for which my Lord did die;
Then in the liquid dome's eternal blue
The angel-wings of childhood's fancy view.

To Benjamin Lamplough,
　　Manor House,
　　　　Flamborough.

August 31.

BESIDE THE WOOD.

A LADY, with a thoughtful brow,
Beside the beech-log's ruddy glow;
A sadness in her soft grey eye
Responsive to her bosom's sigh.

The shadow of a barren wood,
Engirt in snow and solitude,
And hiding one dark form of hate
Foredoomed to Cain's red sin and fate.

A cavalier of courage high,
Dreading no evil, rideth by—
A burst of flame, a pistol crack,
The fair day fadeth dim and black.

A brave man dying in the snow,
Day's twilight brooding sad and low;
A murderer flying far and fast,
Death-shadows o'er his lone way cast.

A lady turns from the log's red light
To peer into the dark, cold night,
That bears upon its frozen breath
The burthen of an unseen death.

To Paul Hunter,
 Hull Literary Club.

SEPTEMBER.

Fair matron! in the sunset take thy stand,
With chastened wistfulness in thy deep eyes,
Gay laughter toned to smiles and gentle sighs,
Responding to low breezes in the land.
Fair face, so chastened by the holy hand
Of God, whose mercy wrought in strange replies
To thy low prayers, sobbed to the midnight skies,
When death took tribute of thy little band ;
Love dwells upon its altered sweetness now,
With wistful tenderness, and gentle aid
For steps that tremble in the fruitful earth,
Whose glories deepen to the burning glow
That gilds luxuriant foliage, doomed to fade,
And strew the brown earth of its Spring-tide birth.

To George Ackroyd,
    Manningham,
        Bradford.

September 1.

EARL DEVON'S LAST LOVE.

When roses strove, as Hall so quaintly tells,
Unto old Banbury Earl Devon came,
The swelling surges of revolt to tame,
And thwart my Lord of Warwick's changeful spells—
When love to dalliance soft and sweet impells!
Whereat Earl Pembroke, with high wrath aflame,
Turns Devon from his hostel, with deep blame,
And thus his soldier's bold love-making quells!
Then fell swift ruin on the parted troops,
Brown bill and gisarm making deadly play,
Ere to the axe brave Pembroke bows his head,
And to the same rude block Earl Devon stoops!
Alas! that love should suffer in such fray,
And sweet white roses blush to battle's red!

To W. A. Greensmith,
    Hull.

September 2.

IN SCULCOATES CHURCHYARD.
(The Testimony of the old Monument).

I stood beside the olden stones,
   The graves were at my feet,
And faded fast the busy tones
   Of wharf and crowded street.
Within the shadow of the rood
   I waited on the dead,
When lo! upon my solitude
   There rose a voice which said,
"I preach mutation and decay
   In green God's-acre, calm and still,
Texts from the cloister torn away
   By the cold Tudor's impious will.
Wrought in the wall by mason's skill,
   I took red stains of deadly fray,
To preach mutation and decay
   In green God's-acre, calm and still.
War-surges ebbed, and day by day
   Time wrought his triumph to fulfil,
'Till these worn relics of his prey
   Were borne from ruins dark and chill,
To preach mutation and decay
   In green God's-acre, calm and still."

To the Rev. W. J. Pearson,
   Ardwick Lodge,
      Hull.

September 3.

AMID THE LEPIDOPTERA.

A MEMORY of wild fen and lane,
    With *Orange-tip* on dancing wing;
Varieties long sought in vain
O'er sunny fen, in shady lane,
    Where *Io* flaunted eye and ring,
And gay *Vanessa* rose again
'Mid blossoms of the sunny lane,
    And *Orange-tip* on dancing wing.

A memory of long Summers past,
    Of thickets where the wild rose grew;
Of sunny days that sped too fast
In golden Summers of the past,
When brilliant wings their glamour cast
    As *Argiolus*, *Acis* flew,
Those treasures of long Summers past,
    Where holly, thrift, and ivy grew.

A memory by each treasured drawer,
    'Mid relics of the beauteous dead,
Of Summers that old joys restore!
A memory by each treasured drawer,
    Of days and friends forever fled,
    Of sunny hours too quickly sped—
A memory by each treasured drawer,
    'Mid relics of the beauteous dead.

To N. F. Dobrée,
    Beverley.

September 4.

SPRINGDYKE.

Charlie, it would have tempted you,
    That charming old, long-lost Springdyke—
With sticklebacks of silvery hue,
Charlie, it would have tempted you,
And dragon-flies of bright steel-blue,
    That cleft the air their prey to strike!
Charlie, it would have tempted you,
    That charming old, long-lost Springdyke.

To Charlie, (C.D.B).

CRABDYKE.

New docks replace the old Crabdyke,
    That scene of mud and fun!
'Twas just the place your heart to strike,
But docks replace the old Crabdyke,
Where eels and crabs, and shrimps alike
    Their lively career run!
New docks replace the old Crabdyke,
    That scene of mud and fun.

To Harold, (H.R.B).

September 5.

THE LILY.

White as the snow the lily stands
　With golden anthers in its breast ;
A sceptre fair for maiden hands,
White as the snow the lily stands !
So sweet it is, its breath commands
　Gay childhood for its happy guest !
Pure as the snow the lily stands
　With golden anthers in its breast.

To Maude, (M.M.H).

THE MESSAGE.

Little bird, carry a song for me
　Far away over the foamy wave ;
For I have a sailor out at sea,
So, sweet bird, carry a song for me !
Oh, little bird, he will laugh in glee,
　For he is my father true and brave !
So, sweet bird, carry a song for me,
　Far away over the stormy wave.

To Evelyn, (E.B.H).

September 6.

FALLING LEAVES.

It is your rest time—frail autumnal leaves
In dying beauty flutter to the earth;
The same parental soil that gave them birth
In the green Spring, their chastened grace receives!
Rest well at eventide—the foiled one grieves
O'er the sad evidence of fruitless dearth,
Yielding no Autumn gain of joy or mirth,
Nor floral coronal, nor harvest sheaves:
But you may rest, as sighing breezes bear,
Through sun-floods soft, Autumnal leaves away,
And day smiles peacefully towards its night!
Yea rest, while gladly through the tranquil air
Child-voices echo from the Sabbath day,
And the old school, by praise and love made bright.

To William A. Lambert,
Many years Superintendent of the Broadley Street Sunday School.

September 7.

GOETHE'S MARGARET.

Did e'er before such weight of sorrow fall
On Innocence so maidenly and sweet,
Flowers blooming round her girlhood's happy feet,
As through life's first fair Summer-path she stole,
To mingle with bird-song her spirit call,
Whose soul, of stainless purity the seat,
Had known no storm of passion or defeat,
No clouds of evil darkening over all
To bursting of the Magdalene's sad tears,
Did e'er a maiden's feet such pitfalls know,
With rending sorrow of such deep disgrace,
Who fell untimely, in her bloom of years,
Unpitied, and condemned of all below,
To read forgiveness in the Father's face.

To W. H. Groser, B.Sc.,
   London.

September 8.

THE WORKERS' HAND.

The praise of the workers' brave, strong hand
Is deeply graved in the fruitful land;
Where towers and ramparts supremely frown
It proves the strength of the monarch's crown.

The flashing blade of the doughty plough,
Cleaves the brown earth, and the rich seeds grow;
When 'neath the praise of a gracious sky
The golden sheaves of the harvest lie.

The crimson hearts of furnaces gleam,
A giant rushes with breath of steam,
And o'er the breast of the stormy sea
St. George's banner is floating free.

Our souls rejoice in the brave old land
With its haughty cliffs and sea-swept strand;
Great names are graved in our hearts to-day,
Leaders in labour and battle fray.

We turn to the village, calm and still,
To labour of wharf and toil of mill,
For praise of the workers' brave, strong hand
Is writ in the strength of a mighty land.

To Henry Hatfield,
  Hull Literary Club.

September 9.

EDGAR ALLAN POE.

On, haunted palace, fair and grand,
　　The glory of a dream!
The treasure of life's holy-land
　　When early sunbeams gleam.
How art thou fallen! On the strand
　　In surges rolls the stream,
As at the waving of a giant's hand
　　Dissolves thy beauty's dream!

Fair Maiden, whom the angels call
　　To rest beside the sea,
Thou art a text of Beauty's fall,
　　Of Sorrow's stern decree!
Above the mourner's weary dole,
　　The moaning of the sea,
Thy bliss of beauty doth enthrall—
　　Love's immortality.

Ah, Poet, Teacher! who shall say
　　Thy sorrow was in vain?
The death-note of whose fevered day
　　Became our spirit's gain.

"*Edgar Allan Poe,*"
　By E. Crosby,
　　Hull Literary Club, 1888.

September 10.

WHEN CHRISTMAS COMES.

When Christmas comes with snowy grace,
   Sweet bells the Advent joy repeat ;
But shadows steal across the face,
Though Christmas comes in snowy grace ;
For love recalls some lost embrace,
   And sad eyes view a vacant seat,
As Christmas comes with snowy grace,
   And bells the Advent joy repeat.

To Mrs. Hope,
   Flamborough.

A GARLAND.

Of buds and blooms a garland bright
   I would weave on a Summer day,
Bathing all in a perfect light—
Bud and bloom of that garland bright—
Until, immortelles in your sight,
   They should nevermore fade away.
Of buds and blooms a garland bright
   I would weave on a Summer day.

To Miss A. E. Lamplough,
   Flamborough.

September 11.

VIOLETS.

Violets are sweetest in early Spring,
　　When the fair young earth is glad and gay,
And childhood, gathering, stops to sing,
" Violets are sweetest in early Spring!"
Violets are rarest when birds take wing,
　　And old folks sigh to the dying day,
" Violets are sweetest in early Spring
　　When the fair young earth is glad and gay."

To Lily, (M.E.H).

THE WORLD OF ART.

Still keep the fair world in your heart,
　　And never yield your artist's love,
Nor let old scenes of peace depart,
But keep the fair world in your heart.
When sorrow hurls its keenest dart,
　　Your art its subtle grace shall prove,
So keep the fair world in your heart,
　　And never yield your artist's love.

To Edward Dunn,
　　　Leeds.

September 12.

RUST, SMUT, AND MILDEW.

CLUSTER-CUPS.

A GOLDEN cup, with pearly rim,
   And golden spores within it!
It flecks with light the shadows dim,
A golden cup, with pearly rim,
As fairies flood it to the brim,
   And taste the stores within it—
A golden cup, with pearly rim,
   And golden spores within it.

SMUT.

A BLACK dust on the standing ear,
   A plague upon the grain!
The farmer eyes with doubt and fear
   The black dust on the standing ear!
Lost is the labour of the year,
   The wealth of sun and rain,
By black dust on the standing ear,
   The plague upon the grain.

To Dr. M. C. Cooke,
    London.

September 13.

WHISPERS OF THE WIND.

Clear voices float upon the wind,
With perfume of lost buds combined,
And sweet old hopes—so long resigned.

These are the treasures of the wind,
Whose dear, low whispers reach the heart,
From founts of joy we fain would find.

Sweet breezes brush the flowers, and start
Dim memories of old joy and smart,
The treasures of time's subtle art.

Where do the sighing breezes find
The low, soft music they impart—
The long-lost treasures of the mind?

By angel-hands were they designed
To deal the treasure we resigned,
And left, alas! so far behind?

Dear long-lost treasures of the wind,
   From Summer fair and Autumn swart,
From founts of joy we fain would find,
   Ye bear sweet solace to the heart.

To *Wm. Denison Roebuck, F.L.S.,*
   Sunny Bank,
      Leeds

September 14.

PLANT-LIFE: A LEAF.

Only a leaf of tissues rare,
By Nature nursed with fruitful care—
Two membranes of tough, flattened cells
Strewn with stomata's tiny wells,
Protect the parenchymous mass,
Where fruitful air and fluids pass.
The midrib, vascular and strong,
In fair venation spreads along—
A skeleton of fibres fine,
That strengthened in the hot sunshine,
As starch within the chlorophyll
Wrought out the life's unconscious will.
Stores of carbonic acid gas
Through air-space and stomata pass;
And raphides in cells are seen
'Mid chlorophyll of emerald green.
Oft doth the under surface bear
Silicious scale and silken hair.—
Only a leaf of tender green
Flooded with Spring-tide's golden sheen—
Only a leaf, its life work done
On winds of Autumn rudely spun.
Only a text of wisdom's gain
Won from the great world's fret and stain.

To J. C. Barker,
  Hull.

September 15.

THE FEVER HOSPITAL.

Where cannon boomed in unforgotten days,
And through a passion of recurrent frays
High freedom, won from tyranny's cold hand,
Wreathed with green laurel the victorious brand;
And the old citadel in frowning state
Guarded the town and port from war's wild hate,
Now stands the Fever Hospital, a row
Of black plank buildings, crouching lone and low
By the dun Humber, with its flood and foam,
Far from the kindly warmth and love of home.
Here come the sick, to rest the fevered head,
Or toss uneasy limbs upon the bed,
Perchance involved in such dull depths of pain
As scarce the old home-memories to retain,
Until their suffering lightens to depart,
And languor feeds the yearning of the heart.
The service of light hand, of earnest skill
The patient's need doth zealously fulfil.
Here once came Cupid to a sick man's bed,
And drove the fever from his restless head:
The nurse's hand that soothed his suffering's pain
Engirt him with glad Hymen's subtle chain.
A pleasant, cheerful legend to embrace
The succouring mercy of this quiet place.

To J. Wright Mason, M.B., M.C., M.R.C.S.,
    Medical Officer of Health, Hull.

September 16.

THE ENCHANTED ISLE.

Beyond the surges of the sea
  A fair enchanted Island lies,
Where life is love and liberty.

It claims not grinding labour's fee,
  It echoes not to moans and sighs,
Beyond the surges of the sea.

Low breezes toss the flowers to glee,
  Bird mocketh bird with sweet replies,
Where life is love and liberty.

All things are fair, all things are free,
  All women pure and all men wise,
Beyond the surges of the sea.

All move to love's supreme decree,
  Soft languor in each maiden's eyes,
Where life is love and liberty.

Where may this peerless island be?—
  Beyond our quest, our keen surmise,
Beyond the surges of the sea,
  Where life is love and liberty.

To F. and M. E. Haselden,
  Hull.

September 17.

THOMAS MOORE.

Soft dreams of Eastern beauty fly
    Like sunbeams o'er the flowers of May;
As smiles precede the wistful sigh
Soft dreams of Eastern beauty fly.
Anacreon's art may not deny
    That wine and passion feed decay,
Though dreams of Eastern beauty fly
    Like sunbeams o'er the flowers of May.

The fierce Danes come! the warriors start
    Immortal in their warlike grace!
Sword-smiths and hurlers of the dart,
The fierce Danes come—the warriors start
To play in arms the hero's part,
    And clasp the foe in fierce embrace!
The fierce Danes come; the warriors start,
    Immortal in their warlike grace.

Wine shall be spilled, and beauty fade,
    Anacreon rest in classic tomb;
Time may the charms of love invade,
And wine be spilled, and beauty fade,
But valour's keen, untarnished blade
    Shall seal the fierce invader's doom;
Though wine be spilled, and beauty fade
    Above Anacreon's classic tomb.

"*Thomas Moore, the Poet,*"
  By the Rev. A. Boyd Carpenter, M.A.
    Hull Literary Club, 1881.

September 18.

MY BROTHER'S NAME.

My brother's name, my brother's face,
  Fair nephew, unto thee belong;
And as in thought I sadly trace
My brother's name, my brother's face,
Old dreams of childhood I embrace,
  And sigh amid lost strains of song,
" My brother's name, my brother's face,
  Fair nephew, unto thee belong."

To my Nephew, Dan.

WIND-WHISPERS.

What the wind whispers, who can tell?
  It sighs to me, it sings to you,
From barren waste, from sunny dell—
What the wind whispers who can tell?
It soothes us like a chiming bell,
  It bids us wild woodpaths pursue—
What the wind whispers, who can tell,
  It sighs to me, it sings to you.

To my Niece, Nelly Lamplough.

September 19.

HEART-TREASURES.

Deep in our inner hearts we hold
　　Sweet Summers that have fled—
Love-relics dearer than red gold
Deep in our inner hearts we hold,
Nor count love's minted coin untold
　　When roses of our June were red!
Deep in our inner hearts we hold
　　Sweet Summers that have fled.

To Mrs. Geo. Ackroyd,
　　　Manningham.

THE TOWER BESIDE THE SEA.

A grey old tower looks calmly down,
　　Supreme above the wild North Sea!
Upon storm-debris, widely strown,
A grey old tower looks calmly down,
Where tides have ebbed and ages flown,
And Death, the scytheman, rudely mown
　　His human harvest on the lea!
A grey old tower looks calmly down,
　　Supreme above the wild North Sea,

To Miss Mary Mallory,
　　　Flamborough.

September 20.

SUNSET.

I THINK of you, and see the harvest-field,
    With flash of steel amid the golden corn,
And many a grace of Autumntide revealed
    As changing leaves upon the wind are borne.
Hedgerow and thicket of wild bramble yield
    Their purple fruit amid the tangled thorn,
As in red sunset o'er the Autumn weald
    You pass, 'mid shadows that precede the morn.

To my Aunt, Rebecca Mallory,
    Flamborough.

SHADOWS.

ARE there not shadows in the eventide,
    And echoes of low voices on the air;
A solemn presence where our dear ones died,
    And shadowy forms beside each vacant chair?
As golden day departs, doth twilight hide
    Dear forms that passed beyond our wistful care!
Unto our love each faithful heart replied,
    And love makes answer to its own deep prayer.

To my Aunt, Ann Lamplough,
    Flamborough.

September 21.

IN QUIETUDE.

Some tones shut out, within itself the soul
    Makes quiet holiday of praise and song,
Nor loses, as the annual seasons roll,
    The inner tones that to their grace belong.
The mind that may not shape may yet control,
    And in its calm the passive heart be strong,
For each life prints upon a sacred scroll
    Some passion of the spirit's right or wrong.

To Miss Elizabeth Mallory,
    Flamborough.

ANDREW MARVELL.

Amid the shadows of a shameful time
    Too prone are we to slip the brighter years,
Forgetful of thy honoured, happier prime,
    When Cromwell, Fairfax, ruled our stormy fears,
And Milton toiled with purposes sublime—
    In stormier days thy scathing wit appears,
Thy hand is open as thy shameless rhyme
    That rang the nakèd truth to guilty ears.

To A. E. Woodward,
    Hull.

September 22.

"HULL LETTERS."

Ah! Wildridge, wandering through old Hull,
What " Flowers of History " do you cull;
Glad gleaner in those fields of eld
Whose mighty forces clashed, to weld
From toil and blood and fierce death-throe
A Nation great in Freedom's law.
Gleaner of words and thoughts of those
Who dared the Stuart to oppose;
To guide the fierce revolt that sprang
From brooding threat to wild war-clang:
That passed from Marston's, Naseby's heat
Unto the awful judgment seat!—
Chieftain and Judge by Death's command
Are dust upon Time's hoary strand;
And you of the poetic soul
Now ponder o'er each mouldering scroll,
To view their stirring age outspread,
Perchance dim shadows of the dead,
As lifting from the page your eye
Great Cromwell stalks serenely by.

"*Hull Letters,*"
   By T. *Tindall Wildridge,*
      Hull.

September 23.

THE DEFENCE OF THE CONVOY OFF FLAMBOROUGH HEAD.

'Twas eventide: we had struck six bells,
When the "Bonne Homme Richard" lay abeam,
No flaunting banner waved on high
Nor to our hail would she deign reply,
Till our guns broke forth with a fiery gleam
Drowning the hovering sea-bird's scream
In the thunder that smote the sky;
And over the Ocean's restless track
The white cliffs rolled the deep echoes back
O'er the long, heaving swells.
Long hours we fought with the foeman brave,
Red slaughter staining the slippery deck;
Far into the darksome hours of night
Upholding the fierce unequal fight,
'Till the dead and the dying strewed the deck
And we lay like a Hell-tormented wreck,
Fighting to cover the convoy's flight,
Then struck to the foe we had fought so well,
But our last broadside was her funeral knell,
Ere she sank beneath the wave!

D. D. LAMPLOUGH.

To Capt. D. E. Hume,
  Hull Literary Club.

September 24.

AN AUTUMN LEAF.

A CRIMSON leaf comes floating by,
    Amid the garden's sunny bloom;
Fair augury that flowers must die,
A crimson leaf comes floating by.
I hear the gentle breezes sigh,
    I scent an odour of the tomb;
A crimson leaf comes floating by,
    Amid the garden's sunny bloom.

To Mrs. Erving,
    Liverpool.

ONE PERFECT SPRING.

ONE perfect Spring we all should know,
    When life is free from cark and care!
When from the lilacs perfumes flow,
One perfect Spring we all should know.
As fair laburnums dance and glow,
    Spring-Fairies in the sunny air—
One perfect Spring we all should know
    When life is free from cark and care.

To Miss Kate Hough,
    Liverpool.

September 25.

COROLLAS.

Only the bell of a floweret wild,
    Haunted of moth and butterfly,
By nectar sweet thereto beguiled!
Only the bell of a floweret wild,
Where *Rhingia* feasts on the pollen, piled
    In golden grains where the anthers lie!
Only the bell of a floweret wild,
    Haunted of moth and butterfly.

To Mrs. J. C. Barker,
    Hull.

FLOWER-BELLS.

Only the bell of a sweet, wild bloom,
    Anther and stigma stored within!
A fairy house, with a rich perfume,
Only the bell of a sweet, wild bloom.
Beetles feasting within the gloom
    On pollen and nectar hoard within!
Only the bell of a sweet, wild bloom,
    Anther and stigma stored within.

To Mrs. R. Napier,
    Hull.

September 26.

WISE FOLLY.

Wise folly be our praise to-night,
  Let humour bear the bells away ;
'Mid repartee and laughter light,
Wise folly is our praise to-night.
Wit's polished shafts are keen and bright,
  The jester's bauble we obey—
Wise folly is our praise to-night,
  And humour bears the bells away.

Life's text is hard, its lesson keen,
  So Wisdom decks itself in smiles,
Forgetting as it bends to glean,
Life's text is hard, its lesson keen.
'Mid-Winter boasts its evergreen,
  November has its sunny wiles—
Life's text is hard, its lesson keen,
  So Wisdom decks itself in smiles !

"*A Night with Gilbert and Sullivan,*"
  By C. D. Freil,
    Hull Literary Club, 1882.

September 27.

A MEMORY (1857).

Ripe brambles and an Autumn day,
   With faces of dear friends return;
September carols back to May:
" Ripe brambles and an Autumn day!"
As through dim shadows of decay,
   In sunset lights that gleam and burn,
Ripe brambles and an Autumn day,
   With faces of dear friends return!

September chases laughing May,
   Old friends are buried in the years;
Sere leaves bestrew the Autumn way,
September chases laughing May.
Pale sunbeams on our green graves play,
   Where life sighs through its unshed tears:
" September chases laughing May,
   Old friends are buried in the years."

To Miss Mary Dunn,
    Flamborough.

September 28.

CROMWELL IN HULL.

Cromwell trod those streets of yore,
When the storm of battle tore
In a hell of flame and shot
As the siege waxed sharp and hot.
Some esteemed him in that day
One who should control the fray;
Sternly hold the bloody field,
And in God's name starkly wield
Gideon's sword—smiting far
On the broad hem of the war.
As the red years drifted by
Was his strong head lifted high,
'Till his sword a sceptre grew,
And his Conqueror's standard blew
Like an old war-galley's sail
Billowing out before the gale.
Then came death in storm and night,
As his spirit took its flight.—
So men drifted round his name,
Some to honour, some to blame.

To Thomas Brown,
    Mount Cross,
        Bramley, near Leeds.

September 29.

MELDRUM'S SORTIE FROM HULL.

Falls the drawbridge. Stern and slow
Drifts the sortie's threatening flow.

Helm and cuirass dance and gleam
In the young day's golden beam.

Overhead the banners float;
Rings the bugle's sudden note!

Clash the pikes, a hedge of steel,
Responsive to the bugle's peal.

Blades are tossing to the sky
As the horse spur fiercely by.

Muskets peal and cannon roar;
Death is regal in its gore.

Onward through the smoke and flash
Meldrum and his warriors dash.

The lines are forced and afar
Drifts the roaring surge of war.

To Major W. H. Wellsted,
  Commanding Submarine Miners,
    Humber Division.

September 30.

AMATEUR THEATRICALS.

But Amateurs were we, and light our part,
Who trod in thoughtless youth the bounded stage,
Foreclosing with life's grief or stormy rage,
To ground on Nature our most tender art.
Unproved, we feigned the sorrow of love's smart,
Nor recked in deadly combat to engage,
Then doffing our war-paint, with humour sage
We taught the tender virtues of the heart.
Oh happy time! serenely facile strife,
That held us to no round of pressing care,
Depicting but some chequered scenes of life,
The promptings of its passion or despair!
With power o'er scenes with joy or sorrow rife,
To draw the curtain, and eclipse earth's dark or fair.

" Amateur Theatricals,"
   By Radford S. Hart,
     Hull Literary Club, 1880.

OCTOBER.

Love girds thee! wild storms breaking on the strand,
Leaves drifting from the brown boughs of the trees,
'Mid stormy gusts and piping of the breeze—
A melancholy death-moan in the land.
Ah, stormy sunset! veiled by wan, white hand
From chastened eyes, whose yearning vision sees
Old winding ways, hast thou no charm to please
And soothe this chastened soul with visions bland!
Red storm-light barring the dim, solemn sky,
Shadow and distance on the long life-way,
Dead, sodden leaves about her weary feet,
Yet finds her yearning soul its meet reply—
Love in the bliss beyond our frail decay,
Love in her home, to make her joy complete.

To John T. Beer,
  Threapland House,
    Falneck, Leeds.

October 1.

KNOWLEDGE AND LIFE.

Give Knowledge! God's light to the mind,
Whereby life's higher truth we find,
And let our common round of toil
Be more than grubbing of the soil,
With one sole end and aim in view—
The gold that shall therefrom accrue.
The unity of brick and clay
Is not the text that fits our day.
Labour and life shall not transcend
The unknown unto which they tend—
That land whose beatific ray
Lights not the ravage of decay.
We toil, thirst, hunger, and depart
From furrowed field and busy mart,
But Knowledge shall the Amaranth wave
And smite the silence of the grave;
Give honour in the common strife,
And dignify the aims of life;
Perchance a higher grace command,
As we approach the silent land.

To T. B. Holmes,
  Chairman of the Hull School Board.

October 2.

THE DEATH OF NICHOLAS FLEMING.

Kings sin, sowing a rough and bitter seed,
Hereafter Harvest comes—their people bleed.
Yorkshire was all atoss with spear and plume,
Red flame-streaks ran across the midnight gloom,
Randolph and Douglas—shredding men like corn
Before the lusty scytheman in the morn,
Ere midday sun has turned his strength to loss—
Smote fiercely, as though God-given life were dross.
Then York's archbishop, with the mayor, took arms,
And left the city's peace for war's alarms.
Priests, burghers, peasants, badly armed, ill-led,
At Myton-Meadows their blood bravely shed.
Masked by the drifting smoke of burning hay
The Scots, a mighty tide, surged to the fray,
With storm of deadly blows, and smote amain,
Winning no laurel while they spread death's gain.
Where war's red havoc was the thickest spread
The mayor and full three hundred priests lay dead.
The rough Scots' joke of " Mitton Chapter " long
Gave title to that triumph of the strong.
Yet they died well, and trust we that God's peace
Was with them in the red hour of their souls' release.

To Alderman Joseph Agar,
    ex-Mayor of York.

October 3.

AUTUMN FRESCOES.

The sermon of a falling leaf,
A red flake on a golden sheaf.

The pimpernel, with clear red eye,
Amid the stubble grey and dry.

A bunch of brambles, black and red,
A violet in its leafy bed.

A clear light in the sunset sky,
An old song dying softly by.

The glancing of a pale sun-ray
Upon a white flower in decay.

A rose-bud on a grassy grave
Where broken fern-fronds droop and wave.

A butterfly with languid wing,
A gem of gorgeous colouring.

The sweet, sad dying of a day
That made the green earth glad and gay.

To Arthur H. Brierley,
  Eccleshill,
    Nr. Bradford.

October 4.

AUTUMN FRESCOES.

GREY-HAIRS, the falling of the leaf,
A low, deep undertone of grief.

The grey of morning, dim with tears,
A haunted eventide of fears.

The moaning of a distant sea,
A weird, sad sense of mystery.

A sunset like a fiery bale,
The shrieking of a rising gale.

Rain-blurred, a sodden, weary land—
Beyond, a wild, wreck-drifted strand.

A shattered bark, a lone grey crag,
The flapping of a tattered flag.

A ruined castle, lone and grey—
An old-world text of dim decay.

Wind-tossed, a sad funereal train
Toiling against the driving rain.

To Joseph Gaunt, F.S.Sc.,
   Dewsbury.

October 5.

A MEMORIAL.

It is over, pain and toil,
　　Long death-wrestle in the night;
From earth's loved and sifted soil
　　Thou hast passéd into light.

Surely God will take for praise
　　Thy dim following of His hand;
Wandering through creation's maze,
　　Lonely hill or sea-swept strand.

Hadst thou idol it was treasure
　　Undefiled of man or art,
All its source of gracious pleasure
　　God's great wisdom did impart.

Lost amid the falling leaves,
　　When October swept the land,
Stacked and garnered harvest-sheaves,
　　Storm-waves breaking on the strand.

Dweller in the still, far clime,
　　Can our voices reach thine ear?—
Toned by distance into rhyme,
　　But an echo from our sphere.

John S. Harrison.
　　Died at Malton, Oct. 5th, 1886.

October 6.

THE SHERIFF OF HULL'S EXPLOIT, A.D. 1515.

Ours was a Sheriff of the good old sort,
Who would the town in right or wrong support:
Strong fisted, brawny, of a manly grace,
The old Norse spirit lurking in his face.
He it was who, with true heart and strong,
Avenged at Haltemprice our crying wrong;
Friars and rustics smiting hip and thigh,
Until in safety's quest they turned to fly.
Hard on their tracks he stormed with sturdy might,
To dare renewal of the glorious fight.
To foil the valour of his strength they sought
Shelter behind their strength of wall and moat:
Undaunted he surveyed their gloomy post,
Reformed and then harangued his sturdy host;
Prepared to salve the burgher's rankling wound
By razing the foe's fastness to the ground:
But ere his valour could the feat achieve
The Mayor spurred up the fathers to relieve,
And by great eloquence and manly art
Induced the laurelled victors to depart.

To John Sherburn, M.B., C.M., M.R.C.S.,
　　Sheriff of Hull, 1886-7.

October 7.

WALTHEOF'S DEFENCE OF YORK.

All York in arms—a mad stark scene—
Blood, tumult, and bright armour's sheen;
Dust-clouds, the arrow's driving rain;
Loud-clashing steel, dark heaps of slain—
The Norman rages, with fierce yell,
The Saxon's axe his wrath doth quell;
Or doth he foot the dizzy wall
'Tis but to meet red-steel, death-fall!
Deep is the Conqueror's wrath! his lance
Points, but in vain, the troops advance;
He sees their valour grimly spread
In shattered mounds, distained and red.
Hope reigns—his warriors darkly pour
Where yawns a breach in the great tower,
And one stern warrior silent stands
The war-axe clenched in his strong hands.
'Tis Waltheof! fall his blows like rain,
Smiting through Norman helm and brain:
They hurtle back—the Saxon war
Floods forth, and drives their ranks afar.

To Edward Allison,
   Hull.

October 8.

THE OLD HOME.

Through long and unforgotten years,
   Wreathed in the ivy's glossy green,
The old home to my thought appears.

Low strains of music greet mine ears,
   As old familiar forms are seen
Through long and unforgotten years.

Glad as the sun that Summer cheers,
   When blossoms bathe in golden sheen,
The old home to my thought appears.

'Mid stormy gusts of Autumn tears
   Its ruddy hearth-light shines serene
Through long and unforgotten years.

As o'er old ground that love endears
   I pause, some scattered ears to glean,
The old home to my thought appears.

Through visions of life's joys and fears,
   The memories dim of what has been,
The old home to my thought appears,
Through long and unforgotten years.

To W. & S. S. Doughty,
        Hull.

October 9.

THE OPEN DOOR.

So baby eyes, in dim dreams of the night,
Have seen the door ope wide, grim formless fears
Filling the child-heart, until flooding tears
Gave sweet relief from dark oppression's weight:
Prophetic spectre of our childhood's sight,
Sad augury of dim impending years,
Who hath not seen the trooping of his fears—
The glooming shadow of an unknown night!
We too, with brows care-lined, in later life
Stare through the darkness of the open door,
Affrighted lest its cavern should restore
Dread forms with which it evermore is rife—
Accusing spirits of forbidden strife—
Too conscious that our tears avail no more.

To Edwin Waugh,
   New Brighton, Cheshire.

October 10.

ARCHBISHOP THURSTAN.

Thurstan, beneath the heavy hand of age,
Drew near the grave that ends our hopes and fears,
The dull infirmities of lengthened years
Calming his pride in life's last mournful stage ;
When lo ! invasion swept with stormy rage
The wild northland, and drove before red spears
Sad womanhood, dishonoured in her tears !
Thereat the old man seized the battle-gage,
And, standing at the altar of his God,
Found grace to help him in his hour of need !
The cross his standard in that holy war,
A long and toilsome path he calmly trod,
Ere dawned the day that saw the warriors bleed,
As Scotia's hordes were scattered wide and far.

To the Rev. R. V. Taylor, B.A.,
  Melbeck Vicarage,
    Nr. Richmond, Yorks.

October 11.

CAPTAIN STRICKLAND.
(Slain October 9th, 1642.)

Died in harness for his king—
Let the sad bells softly ring!
On the rampart, shot to death,
Cheering with his latest breath!
Give him honour, foe and friend—
At the bier our warfares end.
(Cursed chance that British lead
E'er should smite a Briton dead.)
Swathe around his shattered breast
Banner that he loved the best,
Give him honour, brothers all!
Let our bravest bear his pall.
Purest maidens hither come,
Weep for those whose grief is dumb.
With bloom and bud, scented faint,
Deaden the dull shed-blood taint.
Be to him as sisters dear
Weeping by his warrior's bier.
Let the bravest in our band
As his brothers proudly stand.

To Edward Gibson,
    Hull.

October 12.

PENCIL TO PEN.

Pencil to pen, and picture to word-drift
   We grasp fraternal hands on common ground,
   Owning the unity of form and sound
To show the present, or serenely lift
Time's curtain, where dim shadows change and shift
   As each grey-age with regal pomp is crowned ;
   And faithful Nature tracks her annual round
While art bequeaths life's monumental gift.
We droop beneath life's pressure of decay,
   Our last words ebb, an unforgotten rhyme
   That faintly vibrates through the mists of time,
To swell the passions of a later day.
We seize the Summer in her gold-array,
   And fix swart Autumn in her burning prime,
   Beauty's largesse we claim from every clime,
And bear the treasures of her wealth away.
This poem breathes the balmy breath of Spring,
   That picture doth her buoyant youth confess,
Two harmonies that form one perfect ring,
   Through ear or eye the spirit to impress.

To John M. Gell,
   Secretary of the Hull Sketching Club.

October 13.

THREE MODERN NOVELISTS.

Our teachers speak—we stand with reverent face
Before the strength and wisdom of the three.
Mind searchers, who have thought, and dare be free,
And hold their wisdom to the world's embrace.
Not harsh and cold, but touched with human grace;
Nor proud and stern, despising the bent knee;
Nor apers of a false humility
Are they, who dared fresh, troubled paths to trace.
Mistaken, wrong! ah, well! perchance they are,
Who left the track to hew another way.
But may not colder hearts retain the bar—
The stifled doubt they thought to disobey?
We are not of one mould! who knows no war,
Sleeps well, feeds, prospers, nourishes his clay!

*Three Famous Novelists—Kingsley, Geo. Eliot, and Macdonald,
By Henry Best, President's Address,
Hull Literary Club, 1884.*

October 14.

HOME SCENERY.

The still, pure light of early morn again
Brings old familiar scenes, the hedgerow's shade,
Wet grass, light gossamer, and woodland glade,
The swelling upland with its sea of grain.
Far off old Humber stretches to the main,
Warm summer-tints in distance slowly fade—
Calm, dreamy distance that doth gloom evade—
Fair lies green hill, grey hamlet, and broad plain.
When sinks the day, and fades the dying year,
Red sunset flicks the green and blue with gold ;
The woodlands gorgeous in their death appear,
And ardent Autumn doth the earth enfold
Until his passion trembles into fear,
As winter glooms in mist and night, a tyrant cold.

"*Home Scenery,*"
   By the Rev. Dr. Lambert,
      Hull Literary Club, 1886.

October 15.

THE HILL-TOP AT EVENTIDE.

In these calm days you stand upon the hill,
And from the sunset turning, with long gaze
Explore the past, its devious winding ways ;
Its fair green meadows, tracked by many a rill ;
The distant cot, the village, and the mill,
And all life's beauty ! wrapped in silent praise,
That grows the deeper as we leave the maze,
O'er which the twilight shadows, calm and still,
Descend. But yesterday it lay before
Your pilgrim feet, with toil and strife in store,
Undreampt the fair success, the loss unknown !
Now on the hill, serene at eventide,
Your children's love becomes your labour's crown,
Their fair unbroken band your joy and pride.

To J. and H. Haselden,
        Hull.

October 16.

OUR LIBRARIES.

The great eternal hills against the sky
Gloom in the grandeur of their ancient day,
Sublime above the passion of earth's fray,
Their giant-forms Time's change and storm defy.
The citied plain, and sea at their feet lie,
Vast theatres of storm and dim decay,
Whereon the human surge its stormy way
Pursues, as generations strive and die.
Yet our mutations mock the mountain's crest
That vainly echoes thunder of old time,
Our books, recorded thought and life, attest
Immortal life diffused through every clime.
Our monuments—our proudest and our best—
Are our great Libraries—our mines of thought sublime.

"*Libraries: Ancient and Modern,*"
By the Rev. J. R. Boyle.
Hull Literary Club, 1882.

October 17.

THE QUEEN'S VICTORY.

The wild north started to the clash of arms,
Smoke-clouds grew black against the summer sky;
Brave men strode sternly to the front to die,
As wild invasion spread its dire alarms.
To Durham came the lady of the land,
A steel-clad bannered army in her train,
Where thousands marshalled on the trampled plain,
Dared the wild hordes of Scotland to withstand.
Rued then the Royal Bruce his rash command,
His army rent, his bravest chieftains slain,
Himself a captive, wracked with bitter pain,
No more, for weary years, to wield the brand.
Then England's matron Queen rejoiced to see
The smoking, ravaged land from raid set free.

"*The Queen's Victory,*"
To Edward Nixon,
Savile House, Methley, Leeds.

October 18.

FROM DIMLINGTON HIGHLAND.

The shadows lengthen as the night draws nigh;
The sun from western clouds with weird, red ray,
Declines, the promise of a fairer day
When eventide sleeps off its last, long sigh.
From Dimlington I gaze, with wistful eye,
Through twilight shadows, gathering thick and grey
O'er the still village, my long homeward way,
And the old church, round which serenely lie
The graves of those dear ones whose love remains
The sacred treasure of the faithful heart.
Restward I pass. and pensive thought again
The treasure of the tomb and past regains:
Once more I see dear ones who wrought their part,
Perchance in grief, long sleeping off life's pain.

To my Aunt, Helen Dunn,
    Easington.

October 19.

AD ABUM.

We, the later race, toned and tame,
May look back upon the old world flame,
When the Raven on the sky
Stretched his wings of sable dye!

    Ah, old Humber heard the war-note
    When the Northman's galley was afloat,
    And the fierce death-smiter strode,
    Striking time to his death-ode.

The Norman comes with brow of pride,
Spreading bitter ruin far and wide—
    Cursèd be his wasting toil,
    Blasting life and fruitful soil!

Night slowly fades before the day,
While peace follows on the track of fray—
    On the Humber gallies ride,
    Frowns old Hull's embattled pride!

We, the later race, toned and tame,
May look back upon the old world flame—
    With the poets, artist's sight
    See the passion of its flight!

"*Ad Abum, the History of the Humber,*"
  By *Thomas Walton, M.R.C.S., F.C.S., &c.*
    Hull Literary Club, President's Address, 1885.

October 20.

THE ROUND TOWERS.

While you discuss the round towers, I will dream
In light of your reflection's shifting gleam :
Night reigns in silence, dark'ning towards day,
When red-lights round the tower's high summit play,
To gather shape and form, and spread afar
The danger-signal of approaching war.
The roaring of hoarse wrath-horns stirs the gale,
O'er sleep profound to ruthlessly prevail—
The startled priest thinks first of cup and cross
Stored in the tower against war-drift or loss,
Then turns at childhood's wail and woman's cry
To aid their trembling weakness as they fly.
Red torches flicker o'er the high-placed door,
While climb the fugitives from floor to floor ;
And midday sees the Danish surges rolled
Around the solid base of their stronghold,
Where in vain rage they pour the missile hail—
As well they might the solid rocks assail.
As eve draws on, reluctant to retire,
With wassail they surround the bivouac fire.

"*The Round Towers of Ireland,*"
  By *J. B. Williams, M.R.C.S., L.S.A.,*
    Hull Literary Club, 1885.

October 21.

HAROLD IS DEAD.

Harold is dead! the brave and wise!
No more his banner broad shall rise
    Above the sea of fight.
The passion of his proud, strong face
No more the van of war shall grace,
    Our inspiration's light.
At Stamford, like some old sea-king,
    He lightly held the war,
Until our storm-waves' mighty swing
    Surged o'er, and shivered Norway's bar.
He fell, maimed, fighting to the last,
Death-smitten by the missile blast,
    In Senlac's stormy van!
Rent, deluged by the dreadful foe,
Our clinging grip would not forego
    The hope that through us ran:
Great hope that stilled the pang of death,
    When lance and arrow smote,
But left us, with our monarch's breath,
    Whose loss long-warded ruin brought.
Oh, Harold, bravest of our brave!
    We never shall forget
Thy lonely, wild storm-beaten grave,
    Where roaring billows surge and fret.

To Thomas Ormerod,
    Woodfields, Brighouse, Yorks.

October 22.

SHAKESPEARE.

Within the compass of a mighty brain
All time revolved—his wisdom's boundless gain;
While all men moved, the servants of his art,
To yield their homage, and their wealth impart;
Yet less their service than their meed of grace,
Who higher being gained from his embrace,
Who won from dust, and urn, and distant shade
Princes and Kings whose being never fade.
He found a transient grace, a Summer dream,
A dying fame, for genius to redeem.
He moved a lone magician in the earth,
Who raised dead ashes to eternal birth;
Above all Kings and Princes, whose poor fame
The light of genius doth alone reclaim,
He from the sceptre won no meed of gain,
But touched dead monarchs and renewed their reign;
Vain was the storied tomb, the sculptor's art,
He won the mind, and made his realm the heart.
All days are his who triumphed over time,
All lands his home, the lord of every clime;
All fame his meed, whose stature towers above
Each laurelled bard,to claim his country's love,
A king in thought, a priest in potent art
The passion of his spirit to impart.

"*Every-day Life in the Time of Shakespeare,*"
   By *Wm. Andrews, F.R.H.S.,*
      President's Address, Hull Literary Club, 1888.

October 23.

THE FREE LIBRARY.

Pearls for the swine! We make no such demand,
But will to open wisdom's page to all,
That treasures of our cultured art may fall
To those who fail such pleasure to command.
Is it too much we ask? The straining hand
From this outlay no profit shall recall—
Grudged deeply will it be, as pauper's dole,
Wealth's seed, sown, squandered on a barren land.
You read not! Life is money, oil, and bread;
Wife, babes, and pride—a prayer well-said at last!
For used-up clay the common rite and bed;
Life's last resource—Faith's anchor, blindly cast.
'Tis well—and worthy of your heart and head—
Will there be soul to lift such clay at the last blast?

"*The Free Library Movement,*"
   By *J. B. Anderson,*
      Hull Literary Club, 1881.

October 24.

DOMUS MEMORIA DIGNA.

We hold you sacred in our thought, half-sad,
And grieving o'er your fate, whose nobler fame
Still glorifies your unforgotten name,
Whose proud continuance adverse fates forbad:
Thus oft our thoughts reach to that struggle mad
When roses first the badge of war became,
And stainèd knighthood won severest blame,
As high-placed treason its reguerdon had!
Ill-starrèd house, that spared nor gold nor blood,
But nobly served the nation and the King,
With counsel sage, or with strong hand afield!
Until, o'erwhelmed in fell detraction's flood,
What time rebellion's asps were keen to sting,
Thy proud head sank upon its shattered shield.

"*Domus Memoria Digna, a Memorial of the De-La-Poles,*"
 By John Travis Cook, F.R.H.S.,
  President's Address, Hull Literary Club, 1887.

October 25.

THEN AND NOW.

No theorist here, but worker, whose skilled hand
Has dashed off leader, column, and close page,
To calm and feed this news-devouring age,
Keen, if not over-nice, in its demand!
As at the waving of a wizard's wand
The years fly back, we speed from stage to stage;
Our Saint George tames again the Dragon's rage,
Obedient steam sweeps on at our command.
The toil and strain of that old time is past—
Old time that half heroic seems to-day!
We hear faint echoes of the old war-blast
When hordes of Sikhs, grim Kaffirs, urged the fray;
And see old faces, by death overcast—
Authors and Journalists, whose fame knows no decay!

"*Then and Now,*"
By W. Hunt,
President's Address, Hull Literary Club, 1886.

October 26.

HULL COINAGE.

OLD silver penny, with King Edward's face,
Well minted by the unremembered dead,
In half-heroic days, now swiftly sped;
I do beseech your antiquated grace
The highway of the ages to retrace,
And show us—nay, your hands were dripping red—
It might be David or Lewellyn's head,
Fixed on a rusty pike, in death's grimace!
Wise and long-headed, with a savage heart,
To chase your foe, and buy his life with gold,
First butcher of our cruel race of kings,
In what far shambles do you act your part?
Do royal robes your mighty limbs enfold,
Or have they in dull limbo tied your wings?

"*Hull Coinage,*"
  By Councillor C. E. Fewster,
    Hull Literary Club, 1880.

October 27.

THE KING'S BANNER.

Beneath white hands the banner grew
In tincture of a blood-red hue;
And mingling of sweet smiles and tears
Bespoke glad hopes and tender fears.

High-born the chief, and young and fair,
Who shook its light folds on the air,
When underneath a sunny sky
True warriors met to bleed and die.

As the wild play of swords began
He fell, a hero, in the van;
And other hands uplifted high
That banner of the blood-red dye.

Sweet eyes grew dim, and fair white hands
Green laurel wrought in kingly bands,
To lay upon his riven breast
Who sank to deep, untimely rest.

But he was blest: he never saw
The triumph of the iron foe—
That crimson banner trampled low,
The captive King, the headsman's blow.

To J. Milne,
  H.M's. Customs, Hull.

October 28.

THE FATE OF KING EDWIN'S BABES.

Poor babes! their father trampled down
With wide-rent robe and shattered crown,
'Mid whirlwind charge of hostile bands,
Death-clang of steel in giant hands!
Autumn's storm-drift of clouds o'erhead,
Swirl of wind-beaten leaves, far shed—
Ruin behind, death on each hand.
They were borne from the smitten land.
Wailing women and war-chiefs strong
Were with them in their hour of wrong;
Terror waited upon their flight
In storm of day and dark of night;
Short and sad was their hour of rest
Ere they resumed their safety's quest;
And after wrath of storm and sea,
France gave them home, security;
When the death-angel did enfold
Them to his breast, so calm and cold;
And near the altar's gracious shade
Those " innocents of Christ " were laid.

To Miss M. A. Cammidge,
        Withernsea.

October 29.

DICKENS.

In our dark moods of passion and despair
Drifts thy storm-cloud across the shifting sky!
We know the sin-avenger draweth nigh—
Behind the cloud the Angel's brand is bare!
In mild June-sweetness of the Springtime fair
Meek childhood wanders forth beneath thine eye,
Or laughter-tossed, or touched to sorrow's sigh,
Crime stained, or guiltless of one sinful care.
Thy Fates' avenging hands are dropped with blood,
We gloom before thy dark and deadly woe,
When lo! life's sunshine smites our fleeting awe,
Our laughter ripples in a Summer-flood,
Where love, and wit, and grace serenely flow,
And Justice ushers in the triumph of the good.

"Dickens: His Life-work,"
By Richard Cooke,
Hull Literary Club, 1880.

October 30.

EDGAR ALLEN POE.

Ah, Poe! our sadness and our joy thou art—
The strength, the passion of thy spirit-song
Dies into sorrow! Sorrow doth prolong
Its bitterness, and poignant grief impart
The rankling anguish of the barbed dart,
With all the writhing sorrow of the strong—
Unsatisfied desire, tormenting wrong,
The bitter, morbid passions of the heart!
The weird perfection of thy art doth awe,
And hold our sense enthralled to thy command;
Beyond our sorrow doth our pity go—
Thy *Nevermore!* what spirit may withstand?
Held, still we see thee, victim of thy foe,
Yet, doubting, search for stain on thy imploring hand.

"*Edgar Allen Poe,*"
  By *Hy. Calvert Appleby*,
    Hull Literary Club, 1882.

October 31.

OLD LAURELS.

Our battle-fields are strewn on Europe's face,
Our thunders echo from the world-wide sea—
If we have sinned, we have made many free,
Sustained the patriot in our strong embrace,
And poured the rich blood of our noble race
To foster the high claims of liberty,
To raise the crouching slave to straightened knee,
And with great price have wrought his manhood's grace.
We have been foolish, prodigal of life,
Too ready to unsheathe the sword and smite;
To Europe's trumpets we have rushed to strife,
Nor clearly sifted facile wrong from right!
We pause—and thereat clamours fierce are rife,
As vain men cry, "This is the end—our honour's night!"

To Sergeant Thomas Stratten,
    The Hull Submarine Miners.

NOVEMBER.

Gaze, wistful eyes! through diamond window-pane,
Upon bare trees, the earth bereft and cold,
Late clothed in green, and eloquent in gold
That flashed its clear light on gay floral stain.
Gaze agèd eyes! sweet earnestness, half pain,
Speaking the prayer thy pure heart doth enfold;
The city-gates, whose mansions were foretold,
Thy wistful, longing spirit shall attain.
Springs shall renew their bloom—ah, gentle voice!
Whose soft love-lispings reach thine aged ear!
Now art thou charmed to cheerful, glad replies,
With purity of childhood to rejoice;
To lose old sorrows in hopes deep and dear,
Responsive to love-light of those sweet eyes.

To Shirley Wynne,
   Hull.

November 1.

MACE AND SWORD.

The mace and sword, insignia of brute force,
Repellent to high reason, whose calm sway
Perchance shall win a later, holier day—
The evolution of our tardy course!
Still may we backward look, without remorse,
But rather sorrow o'er the long decay
Ere martyrs found the grace to disobey—
Immortal spirit brooding o'er each corse.
The mace primeval vigour doth attest,
The prehistoric club, our boyhood's arm,
Whose selfish vigour wins our honest smile;
But from King Harry's sword we dare protest—
It lacketh valour, honour's sterling charm,
This proud insignia of a tyrant's guile.

"The Insignia of the Hull Corporation,"
By the Mayor, Alderman Kelburn King, F.R.C.S., J.P.,
Hull Literary Club, 1880.

November 2.

GEO. MACDONALD'S ERIC ERICSON.

Ah, Eric of the Eagle face! thy woe
Of hard, untiring mental toil I scan,
Who through thy poverty proclaimed the man,
And won death's-gate through clouds of mist and awe!
Thy mind's high quest proved of thy flesh the foe,
Abridging life's all too-delusive span,
First foiling hope, then bringing low the plan,
'Till sinking strength the laurel must forego.
It is the scholar's chance, his frequent fate,
Who, poor and friendless, struggles on his way;
Yet many win the palm—Earth's truly great,
Whose laurels shall not through all time decay!
Shall not the slain ones, in a higher state,
Maintain a deathless laurel through unending day!

"*The Scottish University System,*"
  By Alfred Aikman, M.B., (Edin).,
    Hull Literary Club, 1884.

November 3.

PLANT STRUCTURE.

Life hangs upon the leaves and stems that rise
From the brown earth, beneath benignant skies;
Yet in our haste we seldom turn a thought
To miracles by light in darkness wrought.
The buffoon's art, light song, and sleight of hand
Our childish glee and wonder may command;
Reveal plant structure, vessel, cell, and hair—
" 'Tis very like fine lace, I do declare!"
We brethren of the Lens, together met,
With "brass and glass," the bright tubes duly set,
Now follow, while our lecturer doth impart
The truths of Science, and his skilful art:
How the keen razor makes the section thin,
Reveals the cell minute, and all within:
The protoplasm's circulation strange
Is brought beneath our observation's range.
The section bleached, stained, and in balsam set,
Reveals green vessels, the thin cell's red-net;
Fine crystals, hairs, stomata, and more grace
Than in the brief hour we can fully trace.

"*Plant Structure*,"
   By Charles D. Holmes,
      Royal Institution Microscopical Society.

November 4.

SERGEANT COOK AT INKERMAN.

Not to the genius of our chiefs that day
Owed we the glorious issue of the fray,
When in the dull, dim morn of rain and cloud
Stole death upon us in its gloomy shroud.
The ringing of the town-bells through the rain
With muffled sound stole on our ears again;
But little dreamt we, worn with siege and toil,
That our foe held us to such mortal coil;
Until sharp rifle shots along the front,
And the loud roar of field guns brought the brunt;
Round shot came bowling the soaked canvas down:
Turned out the Light Division, war's grim frown
Upon each brow, as in a storm of hate,
Came with fierce rain of shot, to meet their fate,
The Russ! We met, and clasped them in their might,
Who forced upon us at such odds the fight:
It was all strength, high-heart, and open skill
That bent the foeman to our iron will—
I saw the morn's fierce drift of storm and fire,
To fall, sore stricken, in the bloody mire.

To Robert Cook,
  Sergeant 49 Foot,
    Hull.

November 5.

TOM HOOD.

Poor Hood! You read his suffering in his face,
The tyrant touch of keen and subtle pain,
That failed to quell the rare and frolic vein
Of living wit, whose triumph we still trace
Where pen and pencil the same art embrace.
Strange that our mirth and sorrow we should gain
Where sickness held so long its steady reign,
With such brief intervals of tender grace.
Poor Hood! His groans were quips to win our smile,
And when he touched us to compassion's tears,
He would our grief with merry art beguile,
Nor leave the "Shirt's" sad song upon our ears;
Or "Bridge of Sighs," our pleasure to exile,
But charm us back to joy, the wiser for our fears.

"*Tom Hood*,"
 By Hy. Munroe, M.D., F.L.S.,
  Hull Literary Club, 1884.

November 6.

LITERARY DOCTORS.

Doctors! Draught, bolus, plaister, and blue-pill!
The silent room, the aching heart and head,
The fevered tossing, rest-refusing bed,
And thousand evils, our remembrance fill.
Ah! but our doctors wield their pen with skill:
With royal wailing Wolcot's louse is sped,
Our nature's human strength by Crabbe is fed,
And Brown bends passion to mind's higher will.
The kindly Garth in verse dispenses health,
On Akenside Imagination waits,
Erasmus Darwin seeks the hidden wealth,
His greater grandson for our need translates.
Old Time, that tracked them with relentless stealth,
Won but the clay, the worn shroud of their soul-estates!

"*Literary Doctors,*
    By A. H. Robinson,
        Hull Literary Club, 1882.

November 7.

ART.

High Nature smote its beauty into art
Through deep love-tremours of the human heart,
That could not brook to let each changing grace
Depart beyond its passion's warm embrace,
But wrought in all its fervour to retain
The fleeting pleasure of its beauty's gain.
The first crude touches of the world's young life,
Grotesque and rude, with nature seemed at strife,
So hard earth-toil and fury of the chase
Made the stern heart its visions to embrace,
Till earth received the fervour of Greek art,
The joy of life that never shall depart
Until the final trumpet summons all
And the last shards of time sublimely fall.
Proud Gothic art, born of the storm and thrall,
A thousand gracious memories doth recall
Of forest aisles, sweet flower, green bough and bud,
The treasure of each spirit-haunted wood,
And where the chisel touched the stone to life
The painter came, with soul-conceptions rife.

" Literature and the Fine Arts,"
  Hull Literary and Philosophical Society,
    President's Address by Dr. John Hare Gibson.

FRESCOES.

November 8.

DEVASTATION OF THE NORTH.

Broken walls, charred beams, fruit trees hewn
Down, and in the dust and ashes strewn,
With broken pottery, plough, and spade,
A universal ruin made
Of home, and all that aids the strife
Whereby men wring from nature life!
Such was the scene when William spread
His giant hands, with slaughter red,
O'er wild Northumbrian field and plain,
After revolt's dark noon and wane!
What matter babe and mother lay
Amid that scene of dark decay;
And sunburnt peasants, lean and strong,
Poor units, smitten in the throng,
Who by their hearths made the last stand
That could heroic death command:
Some few, beyond the border fled,
In Scotland rested heart and head;
While famine, pestilence, and cold
Did forest-refugees enfold.

To Henry Allison,
  Sheriff of Hull, 1887-8.

November 9.

AUTUMN.

Autumn, ripe Autumn! now is on her way,
   Laden with her season's bounteous fruits and corn.
   The dead leaves fall and on the breeze are borne
To earth, and all is gone that's sweet and gay.
The woodland birds no longer pipe a lay :—
   Their last songs cheered us ere the fields were shorn.
   All lovely things that richly did adorn
The changing year, are now in their decay.
Yet beauties of her own she hath, as fair
   As gleeful Spring, that came with bud and song.
Now walk abroad o'er uplands brown and bare,
   And mark the brightness of the sky. Along
The hedgerows, crickets sing ; and landscapes seem
Arrayed in an intense ethereal gleam.

                                      J. R. Tutin.

To John Ganderton,
      Hull.

November 10.

NOVEMBER.

Oh, month of solemn change, sunbeam and storm,
Hast thou no beauty for the poet's song?
Hast thy brief day no high poetic form,
Whose lofty praise may Nature's psalm prolong?
Lies there no garland on thy stubble field,
No faded frondage by thy hedgerows bare—
Nothing that may to pensive memory yield
A troubled joy, or point a yearning prayer?
Has Hope no sacred forms to now entomb,
No gracious memories of departed days;
No cherished type in Summer's faded bloom,
To fill the chastened heart with pensive praise?
Peace broods, November, o'er thy changing gloom,
Thy dim decay gives forth a faint perfume!

To the Rev. W. E. Christie,
 Wesleyan Manse,
  Narne, Co. Antrim.

November 11.

BEACONS.

They're falling fast, those beacons old,
Which once o'er midnight hill and wold
　　The red war-signal cast !
A few old shattered shards alone,
With masses of storm-shattered stone,
　　Bear witness to the past !
When startled midnight took the flame,
And, answering to the summons, came
　　The warriors, thronging fast,
Invasion's wild war-flood to tame,
　　The foeman's strength to blast !

Peace calms the heart of man to-day—
The thunders of the last dark fray
　　Have drifted down the stream !
Our old defenders, warfare past,
'Neath green mounds sleep serene at last,
　　Without one startled dream
Of bugle note, of rolling drum,
And wild war-cry, "They come ! They come !
　　Behold the Beacon's gleam !"
Their storm is past, their passion dumb—
　　Time's triumph is supreme.

"*Beacons of the East Riding,*"
　　By *John Nicholson,*"
　　　Hull *Literary Club,* 1886.

November 12.

THE FIRST SHIP FROM ALBERT DOCK, HULL.

(An unheroic reminiscence).

John F. Norwood, courteous head of the firm,
With whom, as clerk, I spent one brief year's term,
Was not the man to make much fuss about
Such small fame as sending the first ship out—
For our "Odessa," Cronstadt bound, and deep,
First sailed from Albert Dock, with stately sweep!
But our chief clerk, whose head was all aflame
With small ambitions, held it deathless fame!—
With what a fuss he hurried us that day
From Wilberforce's old red house away
To Belle Vue Terrace (on the verge of doom),
And set us to work, in a large, bare room,
Wherein we toiled day through, and long, drear night,
In dust, and soot from lamps that gave dim light;
Our sole refreshment, warm, thin lemonade,
With not a sandwich such small sack to aid.
How he refreshed I know not—but can guess
Hard work or famine caused him no distress!
Kirkus, the honest leader of our weary toil,
Shared fairly with us that long waste of midnight oil.

To Edward Dawson,
  Hull.

November 13.

HERACLEUM GIGANTEUM,
(The Gigantic Siberian Cow-parsnip, grown in the garden of Wilberforce House, Hull).

Green, sturdy exile from Siberian plain,
Where the wan prisoner drags his hopeless chain,
Cursing the freedom of vast moor and wood
With groans that desecrate its solitude—
Happy ye are in exile, for behold
Ye cherished are in Freedom's honoured fold,
Where the proud Stuart vainly wielded glaive,
And Wilberforce wrought freedom for the slave.

To Thomas Massam,
　Wilberforce House, Hull.

ODONTIDIUM HARRISONII.

Harrison's diatom! Prize of old years,
First found at Haltemprice, a princely gain
For the true heart that 'mid earth's turmoil bears
Love for all fruitage of the sun and rain.
O Harrisonii! With what hopes and fears
Strove we those tiny frustules to obtain,
Yet never bound it in the golden ears
Of our collectors' sheaves of fairy grain.

To W. Hanwell,
　Hull Literary Club.

November 14.

OLD MEMORIES.

You move amid the treasures of old time,
   Old memories weave their spells about your way,
And from afar, with low and silvery chime
   Sound the old bells where you were wont to stray.
Again the old town-worthies in their prime
   Discuss, and store their treasure from decay;
Like music of some quaint old ballad-rhyme,
   Their voices stir the twilight of your day.

To Samuel P. Hudson,
   Curator Royal Institution, Hull.

THE PRAISE OF TEMPERANCE.

Thou hast not woven in a dreamy maze
   Of sweet, false words the praise of lust and wine,
A fleshly pander of these later days,
   Or lightly wove in song the praises of the vine—
A higher aim thy nervous art displays,
   Chaste Temperance centre of thy fair design,
The gracious patron of our fruitful ways,
   Whose service tends to strengthen and refine.

To H. Belcher Thornton,
      Whitby.

November 15.

OLD HULL.

Old Hull! Where were you? Up and down
    I wander in dismay!
No ancient bulwarks grimly frown
Beneath emblazoned triple crown,
    Bespeaking ancient fray!
Kings came and went, as I have heard,
And here the tide of battle stirred!

But all seems new, of yesterday,
    Red brick of recent date.
Have you no streets, time-worn and grey,
Round which old legends lightly play—
    Or is it all new slate?
How strangely modern all has grown
Since Charles beheld your cannon frown!

You have one ancient church, at least—
    I hope its not come down!
If not, I'll shelter there, and feast,
Perchance with De la Pole and priest,
    Or burghers of renown!
Here's Peck! his tree is rooted here—
He knows, and will make all things clear!

"*Old Hull,*"
  By M. C. Peck, Jr.
    Hull Literary Club, 1880.

November 16.

PRINTING.

Villainous saltpetre won Hotspur's curse,
The printer's Devil and his ink are worse.
The monks were bad enough in times of old—
To prove it, their old chronicles unfold :
Plain things you'll find therein of king and pope,
Or wicked bishops, damned without a hope !
Nay, not content to write their mind at home,
Sometimes to town, on mischief, they would roam,
And there reprove the King, in words uncivil,
And plainly send his Highness to the Devil !
Whereat the King would scoff, or loudly roar
For rope—when you would see that monk no more.
But when the Printer came, in blackest dye
The sins of monarchs round the world did fly.
Saint Peter's words no longer doubts would end,
His own theology he must defend.
'Twas easy work the King to criticise,
And prove his ministers were great at lies !
Of course there was some little risk of ears,
And Mister Ketch found tough work for his shears.

"*The History of Printing,*"
  By T. C. Eastwood,
    Hull Literary Club, 1886.

November 17.

LAKE DWELLINGS,
(Ulrome, Holderness).

A FRAMEWORK of rough logs, the text of time,
Whose ages dim are like a curtain spread
O'er the rude labour of a people dead,
And lost beyond the legend or rude rhyme
Whereby we learn the glory or the crime
Of those who with their archives grey are sped.
The toil, the passion of their life has fled—
They are the strangers of a distant clime.
The evolution of our higher mind
Still feels the pulses of the savage life
That fed at Nature's rude, but holy breast ;
And lingering love of the old life we find,
In thought reviewing their most stormy strife,
Who found the lake their refuge and their rest.

"*Early Man in Yorkshire,*"
By W. W. Watts, B.A., F.G.S.,
Hull Literary Club, 1884.

November 18.

NURNBERG.

Nurnberg's hand
Geht durch alle land.

Low speaks a dead world from thy walls to-day,
Old bearer of thy Mediæval crown!
So long ago thy ancient sun sank down
With Chivalry's far-flash and feudal bay.
Well hast thou stood and turned Time's sad decay,
Whose shattered shards o'er Europe's breast are strown;
Vain here his ravage fierce, his settled frown—
Not yet thy strength surrenders to his sway!
Not dead thy old-world's realm of dim romance;
Again amid thy treasures of old art
We see the flashing of the Reiters' lance,
The burghers rushing from warehouse and mart,
To face on thy grey walls the battle chance,
With flashing of keen pike and flight of feathered dart.

"*A Visit to Nurnberg*,"
  By the Rev. W. J. Pearson,
    Hull Literary Club, 1883.

November 19.

ALFRED OF NORTHUMBRIA.
(Slain at Ebberston, A.D. 705.)

The Danes had met him in the coil of war,
And from mid-day the winter storm of strife
Had roared and swirled above red wreck of life,
But still King Alfred's helmet shone, a star
In the stern van of his dark battle-bar,
That braved the Northern war-axe, spear, and knife:
With gloomy horror all the scene was rife,
As the wild tumult deepened and spread far.
An arrow, through the twilight cleaving fast,
Smote the good King. As sank his helmet bright
The berserk wielder of a mighty spear
Smote him with fatal wounds. The war surged past
As through low glooming of the awful night
The dying King was borne, with wail and tear.

To C. H. Bellamy, (late of Hull),
    Manchester.

November 20.

CARL REINECKE.

Ah, not the painter's art 'neath God's high dome
With heavenly teaching floods our thirsty soul;
No! it is music, song, the organ-roll
That welcomes us—the harmony of home!
In travail here, by land or ocean's foam,
Low echoes mingle with the tempest's howl—
Sweet drift of song, that gently doth control
The wayward heart, so passionate to roam.
Who estimates thy power on earth's green sod,
Harmonious language of the heavenly clime!
Their faces veiling, at the feet of God
The angels utter praise in song sublime.
It soothes our infancy—life's path untrod—
And with its solemn sadness tolls us out of Time.

"*Carl Reinecke and his Music,*"
   By F. R. Müller,
      Hull Literary Club, 1886.

November 21.

A NEW POET.

This is a poet, dealing with a poet's love;
Soft, warm skies, gay flowers, and heaven's hot sun
　　above;
All flows so soft and musical, in rhythmic ease
The cultured ear with its soft cadences to please.
Here comes the stormy gust, March bursting into June,
Then April's passion of hot tears doth love impugn;
Then Pride, that ever will have headway out of heaven,
Precedes the loud storm, when despair's wild threats are
　　driven.
Is this love? Sighs and bitterness, deep grief and pain,
Ere dawneth, calm and tranquil, Hymen's happy reign!
As through the storm and passion of the long, drear night
Toils the good ship, and finds at dawn the port in sight!
So wish we all good speed unto the poet's lay
With whom we've wrought through storm and passion to
　　his bay!
But now some growls of dull detraction on our ear
Tells that our sage, high cultured critic doth appear!
Avaunt! this is no sphere for thee—Love's realm is free,
Here buoyant nature, not chaste art, holds revelry.
We deny and bar thee out! pelting with posies
All harsh intruders in our sweet realm of roses.

"*Eric Mackay's Love Letters of a Violinist*,"
　By the Rev. H. Elvet Lewis,
　　Hull Literary Club, 1886.

November 22.

JARL SIWARD'S DEATH,
(York, A.D. 1055).

Gird me my trusty armour on!
  Is it meet that I thus should lie?
Bring me the arms I loved to wield,
  And shout the wild battle-cry!

Let me meet the silent Conqueror now,
  In a chieftain's warlike pride,
With my trusty armour girded on,
  And the good sword by my side!

'Twas ever thus we were wont to meet
  In the battle's deadly rout;
Amid the clash of contending steel,
  And the foeman's vengeful shout!

I never quailed at his presence then—
  Shall he deem me craven now
That the palsy shakes my aged limbs,
  And the death-damp chills my brow?

No! dress me in my warlike gear—
  Let him claim a conqueror's right—
A warrior waiting to meet him,
  Equipped as for coming fight.

D. D. LAMPLOUGH.

To *James Wilkie, B.L.,*
Musselburgh, N.B.

November 23.

ATHENA IN THE EARTH.

Voice of the air! the birds have wrought
    Your passion into liquid song.
Low sighs of stormy passion caught,
Tones of the wind! the birds have wrought
Into a harmony of thought
    The joys that to your strength belong!
Voice of the air! the birds have wrought
    Your passion into liquid song.

Hues of the air! blue, purple, white,
    You flash upon the wild bird's throat!
The raven robs the dusky night;
Hues of the air, blue purple, white,
Crimson or gold, in liquid light,
    In fair bird-plumage ye are wrought.
Hues of the air, blue, purple, white,
    You flash upon the wild bird's throat.

Rare harmony of hue and song,
    Athena dowers the waiting earth
With treasures that to heaven belong.
Rare harmony of hue and song,
Fleet flashing of the pinion strong,
    Yours is the joy of heavenly birth!
Rare harmony of hue and song,
    Athena dowers the waiting earth.

To the Rev. James Bransom,
        Leeds.

November 24.

AUDUBON.

In a deep passion, half akin to pain,
He searched the world of Nature for our gain;
And the first promptings of his childhood's love
His grace of ripened wisdom did approve.

Nature to him was tremulous with life—
The unity that broods within its strife
An emblem was of his impassioned quest,
Where earnest toil became the only rest.

Little the world in its mad fluttering
Recked of wild woods, of birds upon the wing—
Nature, the good milch cow of Schiller, gave
The good, sweet food its human stomachs crave.

Methinks, high-priests before the throne of God,
Who kissed the gracious foot-prints where he trod,
Our Audubons devout shall sweetly raise
Strains that perfect the harmony of praise.

Constrained to worship, surely none are free,
Priests in the temple or beneath the tree,
Accepted their true vassalage may stand,
Deep homage to the Lord's creative hand.

Thus in a unity of praise and love
The sacred promptings of our joy we prove;
Thus the fair stars that sang Creation's rise
With Bethlehem's praise shall sweetly harmonize.

To the Rev. F. O. Morris, B.A.,
  Author of "A History of British Birds,"
    Nunburnholme Rectory, Yorks.

November 25.

NOVEMBER MUSINGS.

O for the light of other days,
    When hearts and hopes were young,
When memory could no spectre raise,
    Nor conscience find a tongue.

When life was just an April day,
    Sweet with unsullied flowers,
And all around was bright and gay
    With slight refreshing showers.

But Spring, just opening with new life,
    Though beautiful, is brief,
And Youth fresh entering Manhood's strife,
    Soon finds a latent grief.

For life's unreal at the best,
    A dream of smiles and tears;
No sooner is a thing possessed,
    Than lo! it disappears.

Then shall I mourn my day's decline,
    And darkness coming on?
Ah! no, the Better Life be mine
    Beyond the setting sun.

                      G. ACKROYD.

To Miss Campion,
    Walsgrave-on Stowe, Coventry.

November 26.

AUTUMN'S HIDDEN SPRING.

It is Autumn! sere leaves drift
   To the Humber's turgid wave.
Overhead the dark clouds lift ;
   Sunbeams gleam around the grave,
Cold and damp, and still and dark,
That in Spring shall nest the lark,
   And return each bud and bloom
From its cold and icy cell ;
   Yielding earth its old perfume
From each meadow, mound, and dell—
Yield the new life from the old,
With its silver and its gold,
   With its breadth of living green ;
With its tremour of new love,
   With its flutter and its sheen,
And its shifting light above—
All the glamour of the old
Shall the hidden Spring unfold.

To Wm. Bousfield,
    Hull.

November 27.

DEFEAT OF PENDA,
(Winwidfield, A.D. 655).

Penda, white-haired, a King of many years,
Red to the lips with blood in battle shed,
Again the war-drift of his banners spread,
Smiting Northumbria with a storm of fears.
Little recked he, hedged in with flashing spears,
Nor paled to look upon the mangled dead;
From his cold heart all pity long had fled,
His impious sowing had been blood and tears,
Strewn broadcast on the soil he proudly trod,
Glooming beneath the wild Northumbrian sky.
He plunged, grey chief, as in the days of old,
Into the stormy sea, and met the rod
That smote him down, in dim defeat to die,
And cumber, 'mid his slain, the Northern sod.

To G. Roberts,
   Lofthouse,
      Nr. Wakefield.

November 28.

THE WATER POET.

Taylor, thy life was well and wisely sped
In just accordance with thy Nature's law,
To which enforcèd training makes us foe,
Whereby the dotard's grey bestrews our head.
In youth thy sailor's hand perchance was red,
And Spain thy reeking sword and halberd saw;
Occasion past, the steel thou didst forego,
Thy later steps by wisdom's law were led.
On silver Thames thy well-built wherry flew,
Or wild adventure did unrest assuage;
Beneath the pen thy homely pamphlets grew,
Quaint fruit that found acceptance of thy age.
A loyal poet, to thy monarch true,
Thy head supplants the crown in life's far stage.

"*Taylor, the Water Poet,*"
  By Fred. de Coninck Good,
    Hull Literary Club, 1881.

November 29.

PRE-RAPHÆLITES.

Nature and strength's divinest truth
Met in the fervour of their youth.

Cast off the trammels of old law,
Into a fresh green earth they go.

And there, with love's minutest care,
Copy and show how earth is fair.

As in the heart of Nature's bower
They perfect leaf, and bud, and flower.

Earth's background for life's strength and grace—
Expression of the human face.

That life no more in art may be
A sickly, false simplicity.

But sentient in its hate or song
As love or passion maketh strong.

Not pretty things in china, clay,
The treasures of a childish day,

But life that through the inner heart
Can stirring thought and sense impart.

And call the old, dead past again
To mingle with our joy and pain.

"The English Pre-Raphælites,"
By J. A. Spender,
Hull Literary Club, 1886.

November 30.

YORK STORMED.

Crested with steel and flags of war
The city rose, a broad, strong bar
To fence the surges of the tide
Far-rolling in embattled pride.
The roar of conflict swept the sky,
The missile-shower went drifting by;
Steel clad the wall in glancing light,
Foe greeted foe in mortal fight.
The billows burst—the war-waves drave
In death-spray o'er the struggling brave;
In wild death-glee the trumpets sang,
The swirling twibills clashed and rang;
The cloven mail gaped wide and red
As throat and limb were fiercely shred.
Then in a hell of flame and smoke
The conflagration redly broke.
Hoarse echoes of the death-toil rang
In moan and curse and sharp steel-clang;
Flame and red ashes swathed the dead,
Lapping the blood so freely shed
Day drifted into gloomy night;
The cold moon saw a ghastly sight,
As wild Northumbrian, Norseman strong,
Uplifted high the victor's song.

To T. Broadbent Trowsdale,
  London.

DECEMBER.

Good night, old, solemn year! the deep blue sky
Is bright with stars, that twinkle cold and clear,
Ice gleams upon the silent, lifeless mere,
Snow-wreathe and drift upon the meadows lie.
Life unto death is making meek reply ;
Love veils the sorrow of its falling tear,
Still clinging to the form it holds so dear—
Wan, gentle face ; serene, but fading eye.
Calm is the sky, the frozen earth at rest ;
Sweet bells make solemn music on the air ;
Earth's depth of silence is a wordless prayer ;
Death passes ; gracious, but unwelcome guest
That smoothes the last deep wrinkles of our care—
Affection's clinging grief low sobs declare.

To W. J. Kay,
    Hull.

December 1.

WINTER.

Winter! thou old, hard, crabbèd, feeble man—
For so imagination pictures thee—
Stern, hoary-headed, and with trembling knee,
No bloom upon thy cheeks,—but pale and wan,
Thy reign (for so 'tis ruled) is three months span ;
And at the sight of Spring so blythe and free,
Filling the awakened earth with song and glee,
Thou vanishest—'Tis Nature's lasting plan
That Spring after the heels of Winter trips,
Summer doth follow Spring, and Autumn Summer ;
Still, dear old Winter, yearly comer !
Welcome art thou as truest friend, e'en though
Thy breath be cold, and blue thy frigid lips,
And thy chill bosom filled with purest snow.

J. R. Tutin.

To J. R. Skilbeck,
  Thirsk.

December 2.

CHILD OF THE AGES.

Child of the ages! with the seal of race
    Stamped flatly on thy yellow, parchment skin!
We find it hard to yield thee love and grace—
Child of the ages, with the seal of race!
For scarcely may our fellowship embrace
    Thy meaner form, thy hated, nameless sin,
Child of the ages, with the seal of race
    Stamped flatly on thy yellow, parchment skin!

Child of the ages! have we nought to gain
    From the long labour of thy many years—
No love, no virtue—only sin and stain?
Child of the ages! have we nought to gain
From the long travail of thy joy and pain—
    Thy human heritage of smiles and tears?
Child of the ages! have we nought to gain
    From the long labour of thy many years.

Child of the ages! sharer of the lot
    That binds our spirit to a common earth,
Are all thy virtues in thy sins forgot?
Child of the ages! sharer of our lot,
Shall anger only for *thy* sins wax hot,
    Outcast of Justice from Love's higher birth?
Child of the ages! sharer of the lot
    That binds our spirit to a common earth.

"*Glimpses of Chinese Life,*"
  By the Rev. Hilderic Friend, F.L.S.,
    Hull Literary Club, 1884.

December 3.

SEA-WEALTH.

What is thy wealth, oh, sea?
 The treasure of the stormy blast
 When argosies, to ruin cast,
Paid thee an Empire's fee:
 Peruvian ingots, dimly won
 Beyond the life-smile of the sun,
Though green-boughs shake in glee!
 Pearl, coronet, and ruby fair,
 Dead beauty, with dishevelled hair—
Are these thy wealth, oh, sea?

Thine own dim realm, oh, sea!
 In life most gloriously clad,
 No wreckage of earth's freedom glad,
Need hold in gloomy fee!
 Pearl, coral, and fay-twisted shell,
 Are heaped beneath thy rolling swell,
Where sea-flowers wreathe in glee!
 The many forms of strength and grace
 Which thy dim mystery doth embrace.
Declare thy wealth, oh, sea!

Great wealth of mystery
 Won darkly in the storm of night,
 Or wrought beyond our bounded sight,
Declare thy power, oh sea!

"*The Wealth of the Sea*,"
 By Councillor Alfred W. Ansell,
  Hull Literary Club, 1883.

December 4.

DEMONOLOGY.

Your demon might be made a useful fellow,
If he would only cease to tempt the good,
To nip young Virtue in the tender bud,
And tackle older sinners, ripe and mellow!
Not blight the shoot, but seize the sinner yellow,
Strip off his orthodox concealing hood,
'Neath which he has so long and safely stood,
And flog the rascal till we heard him bellow.
To see Old Clootie clear the mart and street,
Provided you and I were pure and sinless,
Would be ecstatic!—From our safe retreat,
Without one hidden doubt to make us grin-less,
To see the dancing of his cloven feet,
His falling whip, the prancing of the skinless.

"*The Demonology of the 17th Century,*"
  By E. Haigh, M.A.,
    Vice-principal of the Hull and E. R. College,
      Hull Literary Club 1885.

December 5.

FOLK-LORE.

Sweep back the curtain! let the ages live,
And list we to their old, heroic strain,
Rent by the shrieking bitterness of pain,
Or soothed by music love alone may give.
As sand poured through the meshes of a sieve
The ages drift, but of their harvest gain
Quaint, hoarded grains of wisdom we retain,
Sown on Time's dust by ages fugitive!
To prove one life, one nature, and one grave
In legend, rhyme, and dim, age-drifted lore—
Borne to our island, o'er what stormy wave,
From what far realm—we blindly would explore:
To find the language of the weak and brave
The craft or daring of one common mould restore.

"*English Folk-Lore,*"
 By the Rev. W. H. Jones, F.M.H.A,
  Hull Literary Club, 1881.

December 6.

COMPENSATION.

Not man's compensation, tardy and mean,
That gives with grudging heart and cold keen eye
Just what the law decrees—and one deep sigh
Throws in, of sorrow that his hands are clean!
But God's great law, that moves on all, unseen,
And covers all, like His great tent, the sky—
That none outcast beyond His presence lie,
But all are children of His wide demesne:
God's law of love that turns the bitter sweet,
That charms the madness of our wrath to tears,
And gives the calm that sanctifies defeat,
The melody in grief that soothes our ears.
God's compensation for life's toil and heat,
That rules our fretful days, and calms our later years!

"*Compensation,*"
    By C. F. Corlass,
        Hull Literary Club, 1880.

December 7.

A HAPPY YEAR.

A HAPPY year be this to thee,
From olden shadows justly free,
And yielding from old sheaves of pain
The mild fruit of the spirit's gain,
And wisdom's sweet fertility.

Be Summer's twining buds to thee
Pure emblems of prosperity;
Thy life unto its end maintain
   A happy year!

May Autumn, wreathed in beauty, be
A season of tranquility;
And for thy sake cold Winter's reign
Shed beauty on each hill and plain,
And usher in with Christmas glee
   A happy year!

To M. A. Lamplough,
   Hull.

December 8.

HEDON.

Time and change have pulled old Hedon down,
Yet doth it boast some honour of the crown
That shone in older days of storm and war,
E'en when King Athelstan smote wide and far,
And spread the terror of his sword and shield
O'er ancient Brunnenburgh's ensanguined field.
Here rose the castle—tower and rampart strong
Shone with the glitter of the battle throng—
But time has drawn the curtain of the dead
O'er many a conflict widely spread;
And we scarce guess amid the shards of time
How rang the music of the old life-rhyme!
In churches three, bells rung and mass was said;
While monks prayed well, and most devoutly fed.
Hither came argosies o'er stormy main
Laden with wine of sunny France or Spain;
And at the wharves, where strength made labour light,
Great were the tastings of wines red and white;
While maid and matron lightly tripped along
'Mid archer, monk, and merchant in the throng.

"*Hedon,*"
  By *Alderman Park, Ex-Mayor of Hedon,*
    Hull Literary Club, 1884.

December 9.

MOSSES.

See those tiny mosses yonder,
　　Nodding in their shady nook !
There at morn I love to wander
　　With my friend or with my book.

These are friends I often visit
　　Ere the world from slumber wakes—
Ere the early scent exquisite
　　Morn from out the floweret shakes.

Much I love these tiny mosses—
　　Lowly forms almost unseen,
Growing near the pools and fosses,
　　In their garb of varied green.

In the Autumn, too, these mosses
　　Proudly lift their spear-tipped heads,
Clinging round the sheltering bosses,
　　Where dead leaves shall be their beds.

But when Winter comes, snow-laden,
　　Then they hide beneath her pall,
'Till the beauteous Spring, bright maiden,
　　Joyful smiles and gladdens all.

　　　　　　　　　　　　Geo. Wilson.

To R. Napier,
　　　Hull.

December 10.

OLD LOVE IS BEST.

Old love is best ! like ivy green
It clothéd is in gracious mien
   Of changeless faith, and doth embrace
   Our failure with its gentle grace,
As though no failure e'er had been.

It hath no storms, but all serene
Its eventide of life is seen,
   With this sweet text upon its face,
      " Old love is best !"

Old love is like a gentle queen
That moves within a golden sheen,
   And stoops unconsciously to trace
   Good deeds in many a quiet place,
Nor hears this voice in its demesne—
      " Old love is best."

To Mrs. Pearson,
  Ardwick Lodge,
    Beverley Road, Hull.

December 11.

LLEWELLYN JEWITT, F.S.A., &c.

June blushed with roses for thy dying bed,
And shook her fragile vessels of perfume
To yield their fragrance for thy honoured tomb,
When thy brief night of Summer calmly sped.
Tears in thy golden noontide had been shed,
And twilight veiled thy pathway in its gloom,
But ever Love thy travail did illume,
And Honour wove green chaplets for thy head.
Thy name and memory are of peace and love
The gentle texts, in tender reverence held;
Heart-treasures of old friends, whose pensive grief
Finds solace in high hopes of life above,
Where, earth's last sighs of pain and suffering quelled,
True hearts attain the kingdom of their long belief.

To the Rev. Thos. W. Daltry, M.A., F.L.S.,
Madeley Vicarage,
Newcastle-under-Lyme.

December 12.

THOREAU'S WALDEN.

Might I not stray upon the shore,
Beyond the sea's tempestuous roar?—

Many there were within the strife—
Why should I not withdraw one life?

The world's mad roaring had no voice
That moved my spirit to rejoice.

But solitude and nature wrought
Deep praise and sweet productive thought.

The yearnings of my lineage ran
To solitudes untrod of man.

Wrapped in the sunshine and the rain
I had great wisdom to obtain.

Nature had marked me for her guest,
My soul was fainting for its rest.

I went, and touched God's sacred hand
In a serene and fruitful land.

From Mammon and unholy strife
I moved the yearning of my life.

My soul had rest, and tender grace,
Within the sun and rain's embrace.

To the Rev. W. B. FitzGerald,
   The Manse,
      Prestwich, Manchester.

December 13.

KINGSLEY'S HEREWARD LE WAKE.

ENTHRONED in legends dim and old
   We bind the warrior to our heart !
A form of high, heroic mould
Enthroned in legends dim and old,
War-banners o'er his head unfold,
   'Mid burnished twibill, lance and dart.
Enthroned in legends dim and old,
   We bind the warrior to our heart.

Old York bursts into ruddy flame,
   Its grey walls clad in flashing steel ;
As Norman valour waxeth tame
Old York bursts into ruddy flame ;
The roar of battle sounds his fame,
   His helmet heads the battle-reel,
As York bursts into ruddy flame,
   Its grey walls clad in flashing steel.

We see him in the sunset red,
   The stormy twilight of the day :
A hero numbered with the dead
We see him in the sunset red ;
Life's prayer is said, life's rhyme is read ;
   Its dreams and visions fade away.
We see him in the sunset red,
   The stormy twilight of the day.

To the Rev. Baldwyn E. Wake,
   Millington Vicarage, Pocklington.

December 14.

CARLYLE.

He moved amid the thunder of that time
  Of wild convulsion, when degraded life
  In the fierce whirlpool of a brutal strife
Clutched the white throat of bitter, heartless crime,
And shook its prey with passion half sublime,
  Avenging with the brutal pike and knife
  Iniquity that had so long been rife,
Men thought God slumbered o'er sin's darkest prime.
Confounded in the press, blind with the smoke,
Men started back; not murder, death, but hell
  The vision that smote terror to the heart.
But he, unmoved, weighed up the truth, and spoke
Stern words that smote the horror of the spell,
  As Justice moved to work its righteous part.

"Carlyle,"
  By the Rev. John Hunter,
    Hull Literary Club, 1885.

December 15.

THE PORTLAND VASE.

Fair triumph of a long-departed age,
Sleeping through time's mutations wild and fierce,
Until a new-world's radiance shone, to pierce
The grave, long doomed thy pure art to encage.
Unmarred by centuries of storm and rage,
Thy tender art became our treasured prize,
Rich with the sorrow of the heathen skies,
To charm at once the artist and the sage.
In thee the old-world sorrow meets our eyes,
Sickness, funereal gloom, and sacred dust;
The old-world hope that pierced life's dim disguise
To touch, with yearning hope, our higher trust,
Whereby from transitory woes we rise
To that far realm whose treasures never rust.

"The Celebrated Portland Vase,"
  By M. C. Peck, Jr.,
    Hull Literary Club, 1885.

December 16.

AUTUMN JUSTIFIED.

Crimson flush, gold-blazon'd glory
Faded from the old year's story!—
Cold and grey, and wan and sad,
Wert thou, Autumn, ever glad?

Wrinkled brow, and hair grey-tinted,
Was love in your still heart minted!
Did the grey e'er flush with gold,
Ripe and red the lip's thin fold?

Is it but a dirge and groaning
Mingling with the Humber's moaning!
Love-light never in the eye,
Life's sole language, Autumn's sigh?

Eventide's aflush with glory,
Lighting all the old year's story—
Love is breathing in a psalm,
Life is ending, sweet and calm.

Seed is sown and life engendered,
Love's own tribute hath been rendered.
'Tis the husk of life alone
Dies with Autumn's changing tone.

To J. Chas. Storey, L.D.S.,
    Hull.

December 17.

SAMUEL LOVER.

He left behind a subtle grace
  Of wisdom, wit, and frolic song,
And roguish smiles for Beauty's face—
A poet's meed of subtle grace,
Whose generous spirit would embrace
  All joys that unto earth belong.
He left behind a subtle grace
  Of wisdom, wit, and frolic song.

There have been bards who wrote in pain,
  And left a heritage of tears!
Prolongers of our sorrow's strain,
Their words are echoes of our pain,
Where leaves of Autumn fall again,
  In dying twilight of the years.
There have been bards who wrote in pain,
  And left a heritage of tears.

The sweetness of his frolic song
  The Yule-fires of our mirth embrace,
As feats of roguish love prolong
The sweetness of his frolic song!
'Mid legends of the brave and strong,
  Of warrior's strength and woman's grace,
The sweetness of his frolic song
  The Yule-fires of our mirth embrace.

"*Samuel Lover: Poet, Painter, Dramatist, and Musical Composer,*"
  By S. B. Mason,
    Hull Literary Club, 1887.

December 18.

THE NORMAN.

Through a drift of dim romance
Shines the Norman flag and lance,
  O'er the rout of war;
    Arrows swirling,
    Horsemen whirling,
  On the Saxon bar,
Where the broad, keen axes swing
Fiercely round the Saxon king;
And with strong arm stained and red
Norman William spoils the dead.

Well the Norman here is drawn,
With his martial air and tone;
  Roughness of the sea
    In its breaking,
    Now betaking
  Summer's courtesy!
Church and castle builder he,
With his fine propriety—
Ready with his sword in hand
If you tempt him with broad land.

Domesday Commemoration—1086, *A.D.*—1886, *A.D.*,
  "*Historic Notes on the Normans*,"
    By the Rev. H. S. Stork, *B.A.*,
      Hull Literary Club, 1886.

December 19.

TADCASTER FIGHT, A.D. 1642.

SAD it was that they should meet
   Armed for battle, who were wont
Brother-like to kindly greet!
   Eager warriors, front to front,
With the hedge of shining steel,
   Veiling war with lofty grace;
To the bugle's thrilling peal
   Met they proudly, face to face!
Neighbours, friends, whose strong right-hand
   Ofttimes met in hearty grip—
Greeting now with war-command
   Proudly pealing from the lip!
So they met, to part at eve,
   Bitterly, in wrath and pain!
For their valour love should grieve
   O'er the white snow's ruddy stain!
Friends they nevermore might be,
   As in that far, tranquil day,
Ere their hands' white purity
   Took the crimson of the fray!

To the Rev. Canon J. Sharp,
  Horbury Vicarage,
     Wakefield.

December 20.

THE QUESTION.

What have you done this fine Spring day,
   Oh, brown Bee with the golden thigh?
Robbing the flowers in the meadows gay,
What have you done this fair Spring day?
Golden pollen you bore away,
   Touched the stigma, passing by.
What have you done this fair Spring day,
   Oh, brown Bee with the golden thigh.

To J. R. Gordon,
   Hull.

THE REPLY.

This is the answer that Autumn gave,
   The brown Bee speeding swiftly by,
Busy as ever, but grown more grave:
This is the answer that Autumn gave,—
" Ripened seeds where the grey leaves wave,
   Life from the stems so hard and dry!"
This is the answer that Autumn gave,
   The brown Bee speeding swiftly by.

To E. A. Peak,
   Pearson's Park, Hull.

December 21.

LILIES FROM BROUGHTON WOODS.

Wreathed in my song I fain would bring
Sweet lilies of a long-past Spring,
Won from the woodland's dusky gloom,
And lightly lay them on thy tomb,
That their sweet breath of Spring may be
Half gentle praise, half prophesy—
The perfume of a gracious past
O'er thy eternal Springtide cast.

To the Memory of Marshall Bucknall,
    Swallow.

THE VENERABLE BEDE.
(May 26th, 735).

"Write quickly!" changeful day was ebbing fast,
  Night gathered calmly to an early dawn,
The long and gracious labour well nigh past,
  And floating far the evensong's low tone.
Time ebbed, and the eternal, still and vast,
  Impervious to earth's bitterness and moan,
Its infinite and pulseless mystery cast
  O'er his quiet soul, face calm as carven stone.

To James Gardner,
    Bilton, Hull.

December 22.

EVENTIDE.

My mother's friend ! The perfume of old years
Steal softly through an Autumntide of tears,
As tenderly our yearning thoughts embrace
The long lost Springtide of your girlish grace ;
The oft told memories that return again
In winter-stories of our childhood's reign.
Now as our years increase our heart's retain
The later memories of your joy and pain,
That soothéd are to tranquil, chastened rest,
As Autumn sunsets light the solemn west.

To Mrs. Bolton,
    Hull.

LIFE-GARLANDS.

We weave two garlands in our life,
   Of blossoms and brown Autumn leaves—
Twin-emblems of our joy and strife,
We weave two garlands in our life.
With blossoms sweet gay Spring is rife,
   And Autumn comes with golden sheaves—
We weave two garlands in our life,
   Of blossoms and brown Autumn leaves.

To C. D. Ireland,
    Hull.

December 23.

AUTUMNTIDE.

Now from the melancholy trees
The brown leaves float upon the breeze,
   'Mid sighings weird and low.
We own a wistfulness of pain
Amid the cold, chill Autumn rain,
   When with a crimson glow
The sunset lights the gloomy west,
As though for some long-waited guest
The golden gates unbarréd were
Of God's sure refuge from earth's care.

To W. Howell,
    Hull.

AUTUMN LANES.

Merry it is in country lanes
   When bramble-leaves are red,
And trees put on their Autumn stains.
Merry it is in country lanes
As to its close the glad year wanes,
   And gorgeous leaves are shed.
· Merry it is in country lanes
   When bramble-leaves are red.

To Susie, (S.C).

December 24.

A NATURALIST'S CHRISTMAS-CARD.

In what time of midwinter frost and rime
Your Christmas-card brought back the Summer-time;
With visions of Pomona, crowned with seeds,
To sighing of soft winds among the reeds,
As golden, grey, and red the leaves are cast,
The regal tribute of a Summer past:
Though dim, it bears the grace of nature still—
With thoughts of woodland dell and breezy hill,
Where regal butterflies, in aerial flight
Flash jewelled plumes in fields of golden light;
Where graceful ferns their fresh green frondage wave,
And dim, cool waters mossy pebbles lave.
The scented woodbine's tangle of green sprays
At memory's call its faint, pale flower displays
With moorland wastes, brown turf, and verdant moss,
In contrast with the cotton's pure white floss!
Months of snow-flake and storm must pass before
Gay Summer shall its golden days restore;
And you, with vasculum and net, at will
Shall roam by Jersey's shore or breezy hill;
And gain in Summer golden spoils to cheer
And chase the long, deep midnight of the year;
What time the cabinet's treasure shall restore
Gleanings and pleasures of the wild sea-shore.

To Edward Lovett,
  Croydon.

December 25.

NO MORE SEA.

And shall we nevermore behold
   Thy strength and majesty again?
Who wrought within thy mighty fold,
   And won our harvest of ripe grain!

The sighing of our grief and pain
   Thy mighty winds have swept away,
As when the argosies of Spain
   Were rent and shattered in thy sway.

Thy stormy blast, thy foamy spray,
   Hath smote the foreheads of our bold,
And nerved them for the glorious day
   When wild Trafalgar's billows rolled.

The passion of our love and grief
   Are in the moanings of thy breeze,
Our tribute to lone rock and reef
   For death-roll of tempestuous seas.

Oh, sea! thou shalt restore thy dead,
   Thy deep death-kingdom shall be o'er;
And Grief shall bow her widowed head
   Beside thy surging waves no more.

To the Rev. W. Hay Fea, M.A.,
   Mariners' Church,
      Hull.

December 26.

NATURE'S TEACHING.
I.

God's Nature is His holy scripture, bound
In toil and fruitage of its annual round;
That makes unto the heart its deep replies
In undertones and wordless sympathies.

My heart was full of care, and sad—
  I walked abroad despondingly—
    A blushing wild flower met my eye,
And said, in tones which made me glad,
      " Go forward trustingly !"

Forlorn, alone, and cheerless, I,
  'Mid ruins, wandered here and there,
    The green moss that the brown earth bare,
" Remember " said most tenderly,
      " Your God is everywhere !"

While in a region far from friends,
  Behold sweet violets at my feet
    Recall the heart's dear home-retreat,
My childhood's joy—and care unbends
      " My old playmates to greet !"

The landscape brightens to mine eyes,
  That swept the fields of springing grain,
    My mind recalled the sacred strain,
" Though seed be buried it shall rise—"
      Hail, resurrection morn !

HENRY HALL.

To Miss Clara A. Reynolds,
    Hull.

December 27.

NATURE'S TEACHING.
II.

Where gorse and broom make heath's elate,
   And sandwort gems the dusty plains,
   Lessons of comfort are my gains—
" Though sad and desolate thy state,
         Yet Sharon's Rose remains."

Salt marshes flush with gracious flowers,
   With starwort, mallow, southernwood ;
   Rocks bear thrift, lavender, and bud,
To teach the soul in weary hours—
        " Affliction hath its good."

Bogs, where the foot may scarcely tread,
   Bear glittering treasures of sundew ;
   On spur and peak of spotless hue,
Where snow and ice eternal spread,
        Blue gentians rise to view.

Yea, e'en affliction's dark distress
   Bears tincture of a golden light ;
   And e'en bereavement's coldest night
Bears peaceful fruits of holiness,
        And gleams of heavenly day.

Where bees for golden honey strive,
   'Mid blossoms of the vale and dell,
   " Work while 'tis day," their dronings tell,
" The night of death will soon arrive
        To all on earth who dwell."

   (February, 1855.)   HENRY HALL.
To J. R. Wood,
   Hull.

December 28.

CHALK—FORAMINIFERA.

Now turn the lamp up, let its light
Through glass condenser aid our sight;
Adjust the lens, the focus gain,
To view the spoil of cliff and main—
Globigerina's tiny might,
Or *Rosalina*, snowy white;
Mere specks of lime, won from the deep,
To build our cliffs, and fairly keep
The wild, encroaching sea at bay
With product of its ancient day.
Chamber on chamber here you see,
Where specks of sarcode took their fee
With pseudopodia long and fine,
A scientific fishing line,
That won diatom, proteid, ought
That into sarcode might be wrought.
Behold the foramen so fine,
Through which issued each fairy line;
Then turn to section of the chalk,
And hold a long and learned talk
On coccoliths and coccospheres,
The Crystalloids of early years,
And let D'Orbigny's honoured name
With Ehrenberg your tribute claim.

To the Rev. Ed. Maule Cole, M.A.,
    Wetwang,
        East Yorkshire.

December 29.

THROUGH NATURE.

Who loves the green earth loveth well,
   And follows an Almighty hand ;
All seasons the same legend tell,
" Who loves the green earth loveth well !"
For gleaning by the wild sea-swell,
   Or in the treasure-teeming land,
Who loves the green earth loveth well,
   And follows an Almighty hand.

His sermons are in brooks and stones,
   In buds and leaves of gentle Spring ;
His psalms are in the wild-bird tones,
His sermons in the brooks and stones—
He finds his text in burs and cones,
   And in the butterfly's gay wing ;
His sermons are of brooks and stones,
   Of buds and leaves of gentle Spring.

Each desert blossoms with the rose,
   And sheds a fragrance on the gale ;
Though shades of evening gloom and close,
Each desert blossoms with the rose !
Each sunbeam doth a world disclose,
   He finds a temple in each vale,
As deserts blossom with the rose,
   And waft their fragrance on the gale.

To the Rev. Richard Green,
   Didsbury College,
      Manchester.

December 30.

WINTER FRESCOES.

Dim breaking of a fruitless day
In its sad cerecloth of decay.

A wild moor scourged with wind and hail,
A lone tree swaying in the gale.

The dark breast of an inky sea
Held in dim bonds of mystery.

A snow-white pall, a clear-blue sky,
A cheerful woodman whistling by.

An old church garbed in ivy green
Looks down upon the wintery scene.

A bright star rises in the sky—
The Lord Christ's birthday draweth nigh.

Glows holly red and mistletoe
Against a world of Winter snow.

Through breaking of the frozen earth
A fair white snowdrop peeps to birth.

*To Albert Ernest Ellison, R.D.S. (Eng.,) F.S.A. (Lon.,)
Bradford.*

December 31.

WAITING IN WAR-TIME.

Winter glooms of the dying year
Overwrap the Humber, cold and drear.
Labour ceases—wind and snow
Dash and mingle above, below!
Wind-gusts whirling, shrieking afar
Like madmen 'neath the scourge of war!
Hull is waiting—the war-clouds dense
Deeply thicken to gloom intense.
Little of mirth, little of cheer,
Light the shades of the dying year.
Eyes of women flash and startle
Seeking war in Yule-log's sparkle.
Anxious thought leads them far away
Where Hanson heads the thickening fray!
Starting arrows and the red steel
Dash and gleam in the battle reel,
Till with the close of the dying day
Briefly ends the murderous fray!
Frozen corpses on Wakefield-green
Amid the snow-slush red are seen!

To A. J. Newton,
  Northwood,
    Chislehurst, Kent.

A RETROSPECT OF THE YEAR.

Hope dashed the grey of the glad New Year,
Spring smiled through the woe of Winter's tear:
The snowdrops peeped through the frozen earth,
The meek, fair promise of fuller birth.

Spring, with its breezes of sturdy health,
Clothed the brown branches with budding wealth:
Pale primroses starred the soft green grass,
Where fuller life of the year should pass.

Queen Summer, sweet conqueror! seized the land;
It blushed to life at her mild command:
A tangle of herbage, bloom, and bud,
Bathed in the wealth of the hot sun-flood.

Swart Autumn strode through the cornland wide,
Garnering fruit in his kingly pride:
Winged storm-clouds swept o'er the cold blue sky,
The woods were regal in russet dye!

King Winter breathed on the cold, chill air,
The earth lay naked, and brown, and bare:
The winding sheet of the snow swept down,
As Christmas smiled 'neath his holly crown.

To J. O. Lambert,
  Hessle.

THE OLD YEAR.

Old year! thou art the victor! thy cold hand
   Has touched to smite and still the grieving heart,
   In life's last agony to quell its smart,
And write sad epitaphs upon the sand.
Dim shadows fall upon our twilight land,
   Old memories with the vanished dead depart,
   Enshrined, how vainly! by Affection's art,
As wild, erosive billows sweep the strand.

Old year! departed with thy storm and change,
We will not load thee with our heavy blame,
For hope deferred, lost love, or thwarted aim,
Or life's eclipse within thy circling range;
But own, although thy dealings have been strange,
Thou hast been true unto thine olden fame,
In May or grim December still the same,
With smile or frown o'er dusty street or grange
Where nature, with a long and glad embrace,
Gives beauty to the sorrow of decay!
Storm-born, to leave us with December-days,
Hast thou not left us dreams of Summer grace,
Autumnal gold o'er dim November's grey,
Life's far horizon pierced by sunset rays?

To the Rev. John Charteris Johnston,
    Leeds,

MEMORY-FRESCOES.

Old roof, you nevermore will be
    The refuge of my heart again,
As in the Springtide of life's glee!
Old roof, you nevermore will be
The home where I was wont to see
    Dear faces touched with love and pain;
For nevermore your roof will be
    The refuge of my heart again.

Old Winter beats the cottage pane,
    The world is dark and cold without:
Old memories mingle with the strain
That Winter beats upon the pane—
I see a friendly face again
    And turn awhile from Cooper's Scout,
As Winter beats the cottage pane—
    The world is dark and cold without!

Old memories of a Christmas eve
    In Springtide of a waning life!
Old love, old friendship I receive
In memories of a Christmas eve.
Again o'er Cora's death I grieve,
    As Uncas bleeds beneath the knife—
Old memories of a Christmas eve
    In Springtide of a waning life!

To Geo. Robinson,
    Middlesbro'.

www.ingramcontent.com/pod-product-compliance
Lightning Source LLC
Chambersburg PA
CBHW030427300426
44112CB00009B/892